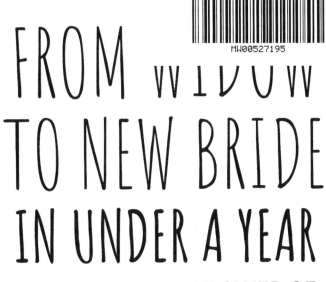

FROM WIDOW
TO NEW BRIDE
IN UNDER A YEAR

THE RESTORATIVE POWER OF

GOD'S
LOVE

LARISA WILSON

A wholly owned subsidiary of TBN

This book is dedicated to Pastor Sal Maiorana, who gave me the idea to write this book, and to Bob Wilson, who gave me the courage and confidence to write it.

For Debbie, I wish you were here to read this...

TABLE OF CONTENTS

FOREWORD

I have the privilege of going to the same church as Larisa, the Waymart Church. I have had the opportunity to see people who really have a heart for Christ and genuinely want to do God's work, and I have seen that in Larisa. Anyone who meets or talks to Larisa can feel something different about her. You can't help but love her. She could have easily let the death of her husband destroy her and end up being bitter and pulled away from God. Instead, she took her time to mourn, and then she pulled herself up and figured out a way to not let her pain hinder God's plan for her life. She then made it her mission to use her tragedy to help others. That is what you read and feel throughout this book.

I am a licensed professional counselor, and I have worked in all aspects of mental health care throughout my thirty-plus-year career. I am always looking for resources to help my patients that are going through various types of loss or trauma. This book will be a resource that I will use, and I believe it will benefit those who read it.

This book will make you cry, laugh, and rejoice in what God can do in our lives in the midst of tragedy. Larisa wrote in such a way that you can feel the emotions on every page and feel every step of her journey of healing, resilience, and restoration. I was able to feel the raw sadness and despair at the time of her husband's death. I was also able to feel the comfort she experienced from

God's love and strength when she thought she had none. I felt myself rejoicing with her as she received God's blessing of restoration when she believed in God's promises. She was able to convey in a faithful way that God is in control, and we are not. Larisa was masterful at showing us how blessing came out of her tragedy. Because her writing is so raw and real, it drew me in, and I did not want to stop reading.

I have no doubt that this book can help others that have gone through or are currently going through a traumatic time in life. I have never gone through the death of a spouse, but I can relate what I read in this book to other difficult times in my life and use a steadfast faith and trust in God to get me through those times, as Larisa shared. Once you start reading, you will not want to put it down!

Thank you, Larisa, for sharing your painful, sorrowful, beautiful, and blessed life with all of us!

Your friend and sister in Christ…

Jeanie Coles, PhD, MS, Licensed Professional Counselor

National Board Certified Counselor, Certified Anxiety Treatment Specialist

PREFACE

The fact that you are picking up this book and reading it is not an accident! I believe that this story of my experience can be used as a tool to help, encourage, and point people directly to Jesus and how to have a relationship with Him or how to improve your relationship with Jesus beyond your wildest dreams! I don't know how this book fell into your hands, but I am convinced that it is something that God wants you to read. It is my hope and prayer that my story will help you to have a close and/or closer relationship with the creator of the universe. May today, as you pick it up and begin to read it, be the beginning of a journey for you into a relationship with the one who loves you and created you! Again, I say that I believe that it is not an accident that you are reading this book! May God bless you and speak to you as you read! Enjoy!

—**Larisa Wilson**

This is my journey with God, from the death of my first husband to the marriage of my second husband.

"My life is an example to many, because you have been my strength and protection" *(Psalm 71:7).*

CHAPTER 1: JANUARY

It is only by the grace of God that we wake up in the morning, go through our day, and are able to lay back down in our own beds at night and go to sleep. No one is more acutely aware of this than I am. This was the furthest thing from my mind, however, as I went to work Wednesday morning and said to my husband, Rich, "See you tonight," as I walked out the door, got into my car, and drove to my job. How was I to ever guess that it would be the last time I would see him alive, and yet it was. As he took our son, fifteen, and daughter, thirteen, to school and dropped them off, they also had no idea. Rich himself also had no idea that today would be the day he would depart his life here on Earth and be ushered into the presence of Jesus, and yet...today was the day.

It was only about fifteen minutes after I got home from work that I got the phone call. To be honest, I don't even know why I answered my cellphone because it was a number I did not even recognize, and I usually do not answer calls from unknown sources, and yet I did.

It was my nephew, and immediately I got a bad feeling as I heard the tone of his voice, telling me to get to the hospital. He had told me that Rich had "passed out." I drove with my daughter on the way to the hospital, furiously praying that Rich would be okay. When I got to the hospital and saw the look on my nephew's face, dread began to well up inside me, and yet I still refused, could not possibly believe that anything really bad had happened to Rich.

There is no need to go into details, but suffice it to say, as I was escorted into the ER, I saw doctors and nurses working on what was an obviously lifeless form of Rich. I immediately went into shock. I remember holding his hand and feeling how cold it was. I remember looking into his lifeless face and the horror I felt at seeing death up-close in the face of a person I loved. I remember thinking how awful, how wrong it felt, how completely it was against any kind of existence where there was a God who loved us and cared for us. How could this possibly be? Was I a Christian? Yes. Was I a Christian for a long time? Yes. Did I really and truly believe in God and Jesus Christ as my Savior? Yes. And yet, it almost came crashing down around me.

I say "almost" because it did not completely come crashing down, it came close, but it did not. Because deep down inside of me, in the middle of the horror and the shock, I knew that my relationship with Jesus was, in fact, real; it was genuine. My faith was barely hanging on by a thread, but it was there.

The time at the hospital spent with family, friends, and my pastor was all a blur. The shock of what had happened was almost more than what my brain could handle and understand. I kept feeling like I was going to pass out. Seeing the anguish on the faces of those that loved Rich further deepened my pain. The disbelief on their faces mirrored my own. I'll never forget my sister-in-law on her knees in front of me, holding me as we recited the Lord's prayer together.

The ride home was a blur as well, but when I walked into my house with my children, it really hit me hard; Rich was gone. I wandered through the house, looking at his clothes, the things that he would never touch or use again. I just couldn't believe it; I couldn't believe that God had done this to me! As I continued to wander around in shock, even with all the pain I was in, I felt something else. I could feel a presence with me, an unseen presence. As I finally sat down in exhaustion, I felt as though there was a person sitting down with me and putting His arm around me. It was such a strong feeling that it almost felt physical. At that point, I knew, I really knew, that I was not alone. I knew it was the presence of Jesus. It was the strongest wave of peaceful feeling that I had ever experienced in my entire life. I could tell that what I was feeling was not of this world. It was much larger and more powerful than that. And as upset as I was that my heavenly Father had allowed this, I felt comforted that He was there with me. And I wanted Him there.

Have you ever been blindsided? Have you ever had

the carpet ripped out from underneath you? Have you ever been thrust into a horrifying situation that there was no way you could have ever been prepared for? Psalm 34:18 tells us, "The Lord is close to the brokenhearted; he rescues those whose spirits are crushed." I can assure you that this is true, especially if you are a believer. God the Holy Spirit is within you, God Himself is omnipresent, He is everywhere, but He is especially close to those who are grieving. I really don't know and can't explain how He can be so close to us but be even closer to us in our grief, but He is, and I have experienced this first-hand! His presence was not just there, but really there, almost like a physical presence; I could almost feel His arm around me. I knew Jesus was holding me like we as parents would hold our children when they are brokenhearted. I knew my grief did not go unnoticed; I knew God was there, was concerned, was loving me, holding me, and sustaining me. I would not have even survived that first night if it wasn't for Him.

If you are reading this and not sure if you have a relationship with Jesus, or not even sure if this "God thing" is even real, I would encourage you to consider this; that God does exist and that He does indeed love *you*! It's true! He created you, made you in *His* image, made you unique, made you like no other, and *He* loves you! He loves you more than anyone else has or ever will! Ephesians 1:4–5 says,

> *Even before he made the world, God loved us*
> *and chose us in Christ to be holy and without*

fault in his eyes. God decided in advance to adopt us into his own family by bringing us to himself through Jesus Christ. This is what he wanted to do, and it gave him great pleasure.

Now read that again, and put yourself into that equation!

"Even before He made the world, God loved *me*, God chose *me*, God decided in advance to adopt *me* into His family through Jesus Christ! This is what He wanted to do for *me*!"

Further on, in chapter 3 it says,

Christ will make his home in your hearts as you trust in him. ...And may you have the power to understand, as all God's people should, how wide, how long, how high, and how deep his love is. May you experience the love of Christ, though it is too great to understand fully.

Ephesians 3:17–19

God's love is way too great for us to understand, but it is true, it is real, and it is there, and it is *there for you* if you believe and accept it!

CHAPTER 2: FEBRUARY AND MARCH

Jeremiah 29:11 says, "'For I know the plans I have for you,' says the Lord. 'They are plans for good and not for disaster, to give you a future and a hope.'"

And this is the verse that I could not get out of my mind as I began my dark journey through widowhood. I woke up every morning shattered and grieving. I could barely handle watching my children go through the pain of losing their father. The shock of it all was numbing and paralyzing. It was almost more than I could bear. And this verse in Jeremiah kept popping into my head, and I kept asking myself, "How could this be? This is the plan God has for me? This is the 'good' plan He has for me? This is my 'future'? This is my 'hope'? Are you kidding me?"

I thought this verse did not apply to me. It applied to some people, but not everyone. Some people have good lives, and some do not. I thought that these were the cards that I had been dealt, and there was nothing I could do about it. I would be lying if I said I wasn't angry with God because I was.

I had been a believer from a young age, but, unfortunately, I had spent most of my early years not wanting much to do with God. When I met and married Rich, I was starting to get back on track and rebuild my relationship with God. Rich was not a true believer in Jesus as his Savior, but I thought I could be a good influence on him, and he would become one. That did not go as planned. What actually happened is that it started to cause a rift between us, especially as I was growing closer to God.

We had jumped around to different churches over the years and attended sporadically when God led us to The Waymart Church. It was truly divine intervention and the best thing that could have happened to either one of us. It was the place where Rich found Jesus and began a personal relationship with Him, and it was where I finally found a home, a spiritual family, and a new passion for Jesus.

We had been attending there for a year and a half, and it was wonderful to see the change in Rich over that time, so I could not understand, after that short period of time, how God could have taken him. "Why now, God?" I would ask, "Why now?" I thought God had big plans for him. I didn't know how I could have been so wrong about that. The verse in Jeremiah kept popping into my head. Was this the "good" plan He had for Rich? Was this his hope and future? Obviously, I was so thankful that Rich knew Jesus and that he was in His presence right now, but on the other hand, I felt that there was something so wrong with him being taken away from his life, his family, and the place he loved so much.

It truly was the knowledge that Rich was with Jesus that gave me peace, but I still couldn't help but wonder why God chose to take him when he had finally just started to understand Jesus' love for him and loved and served Him in return.

I also could not understand how God could have done this to *me* just as I was finally, after many years, starting to understand how much Jesus loved *me*, and I really started to love *Him* and serve *Him*. Even as I am writing this, I can see how selfish and self-absorbing this sounds, but that was how I felt at the time, that this was something that God had personally done to *me*.

My feelings fluctuated between shock and anger. I was still in so much shock over what had happened because it was so unexpected and really just came out of the blue, and I really could not believe the fact that I was a widow at fifty years old. I never saw it coming.

When I was not in shock, I was angry at God. I knew that everything in life goes according to His perfect plan, but I could not, for the life of me, figure out how this could have been His perfect plan for my children and me. I now had to live life alone? I now had to take care of a house and raise two teenagers alone? I now had to assume all house duties alone? And what about my children? They now had to live their lives without a dad, a dad they adored? They now had to go on for the rest of their lives with broken, shattered hearts? They now had to go on throughout high school, sports, graduations, jobs, etc., watching all of their friends have dads to cheer them on but not have a dad of their own anymore?

In the midst of all of this, I have to mention the love of brothers and sisters in Christ who poured out their love all over my family and me. The cards, prayers, gifts, and food that were sent my way were positively overwhelming. Not only was God pouring out His love over me in massive waves through the Holy Spirit, but He was pouring out His love over me through the loving acts of my brothers and sisters in Christ. I have to tell you, fellow believers, that when you send a meal, a card, a text, a prayer out to someone else who is having a hard time, you have no idea—*no idea*—how much it means to that person! So many times, I felt like I was drowning, and it was that card, that text, that kind word that pulled me up out of the waters of grief and helped me get my bearings! Always keep it up! When God lays someone on your heart, take action! Pray for them, call them, send them a card or a text. You literally could be saving someone's life.

I specifically remember a family that came to visit one week after Rich died, and they brought my family food. While they were there, the husband prayed for all of us. I will never forget this moment, and it is seared into my heart and mind forever. While praying, he said, "May You reveal Yourself to this family mightily." I remember that at that moment, I got goosebumps, and I felt as if something really important had just been said. It was something that, up until that point, I had not heard anyone pray for me. It was something that set my heart racing and put a fervent desire in my heart. I echoed his prayer in my heart continuously, even as he kept on praying.

Yes, Lord! my heart cried. *Reveal Yourself to me! I want to see You, to know You, to feel You like I never have before!* It was longing as I had never felt before in my life. I had been a believer for a long time, and there were times in my life when I really felt the Lord's presence, but I know that God never revealed Himself to me, certainly not in a "mighty" way! I never knew Him *intimately.* This was always because of *me* and not *Him*, as He was *always* there, but I was the one who had kept Him at arm's length. I knew that my relationship with God should have been the closest, most important relationship in my life, and yet it was not. I had relationships with friends and family members that were much more intimate than my relationship with God.

It was at that point that I realized that I wanted and needed God. I wanted, needed, and desired Him more than anything else in my life. This was not just because of what had happened to Rich, because I know that, for the last two years, I was growing closer and closer to God and seeking Him out more. But this was the event that made everything come together. I literally had nowhere else to go but to God. This was where the rubber was going to meet the road, so to speak. This was where I was going to find out if my faith was real or not. This was the moment of "do or die."

If you are a believer and, like me, you never had a

truly close and intimate relationship with God, please let *now—today—*be the day that you start! You know, there are believers, and there are Jesus followers. There are Christians that are, shall we say, not entirely committed to living for Christ. That is what I was. They may go to church every Sunday, they may pray a little prayer every night before they go to bed, and they may use the proper Christian "lingo," but their lives seem to be not really that much different than unbelievers. They attempt to read their Bible every day but do not attempt to apply it to their own lives. They post the cute little inspirational memes on their social media but have no idea how to live it. I am not judging anyone who does these things because, you see, I did all of those things, but I was missing out. I was not a true Jesus follower.

You know what I'm talking about, the true *Jesus followers*, the ones who have a personal, intimate relationship with God, the ones who are almost annoyingly *joyful*, the ones always with a smile on their face and a "Praise the Lord" on their lips. The first ones to step up when there is a need in the church or with a family. The ones that when they are speaking about God, can barely control their excitement! That was not me. That was not something I thought I would ever be.

Does this make sense? Do you understand what I am trying to say? There are believers, and there are *Jesus followers*. Do not get me wrong or misunderstand; both are believers, both are Christians, and both are children of God. But…there is something distinctly different between believing that Jesus died for your sins and that someday when you die, you will go to heaven, and then living your life completely for Jesus because of that fact! There is a difference between believing and living, from knowing and acting it out in your life. I must admit that for the first half of my life, I was a believer, and now for the second half of my life, however long it may be, I will be a follower of Jesus! I will no longer live my life the way I want to by simply believing that Jesus is my Savior; I will now live out my life exclusively for *Him* and for *His* glory *because* He is my Savior! I will live my life to show others just how *wonderful* and *amazing* it is to have an intimate relationship with your creator! I will live to show others the *love* that Jesus has for them, and I will live to show others that no matter who they are or whatever their circumstances might be, they are *loved* more than they can ever know! And I can tell you; there is no comparison between the two! Being someone who believes in Jesus but doesn't think that it makes much of a difference in your life kind of doesn't make sense. But being a Jesus follower that believes in Jesus and that knowing Him is a truly life-changing experience is something completely different. It is a life that is filled with *joy* and *peace* and *power* that is so great that you can barely contain yourself most days! It is *overwhelming* and *exciting* and can help you be able to do things that you *never thought possible*!

This book is a journey of what I went through from being a believer to becoming a true follower of Jesus Christ. It is not something that happens overnight; it is a journey of faith, patience, self-discovery, and most importantly, *God-discovery*. It is my hope and prayer that as you read this book, dear believer, it will encourage you and inspire you to really consider what it would take to really and truly know God in an intimate way and that it is a step that you would want to take! It is also my hope and prayer that it is something that you would *want* to do and do now. Don't wait until a tragedy has to happen for you to really seek out God and find out exactly who He is, how wonderful He is, and how *great* His love is for you!

If you are reading this, and you are not sure if you believe, this may all seem so foreign to you! It may even seem a little crazy. And in a way, it is crazy, at least from the world's point of view. The world simply cannot understand how a person can have such joy and peace, especially in the middle of a tragedy, illness, or dire circumstances. You can talk all you want about the power of positive thinking, simplifying your life, or dozens of ways that the world tells you that you can have a perfect life, but all of that only goes so far. It is like taking a 1,000-gallon void in your life and filling it with 300 gallons. So much of the advice is good and helpful but does not complete you like a relationship with the creator of the universe does.

A true relationship with God is a crazy life, and I mean that in the best way possible. It is filled with crazy joy, crazy peace, and unfathomable happiness that is beyond our understanding! It is a wild ride! I hope and pray that you will be intrigued enough to continue reading this book and that it may be the first step in your journey to knowing the God of the universe who loves you so much and wants to have an intimate relationship with you!

And so, with that prayer that my friend prayed, I begin my own journey to know the creator of the universe, the lover of my soul, more intimately. It began as a small, smoldering ember deep in my soul. It was barely perceptible and certainly not obvious to anyone around me, but I knew it was there. And I had no idea what was in store for me in the next weeks and months to come. First Corinthians 2:9 says, "No eye has seen, no ear has heard, and no mind has imagined what God has prepared for those who love him"!

I also want to mention another prayer that my pastor prayed for me that had become my mantra in the weeks and months to come. This was a prayer that I had heard him mention before in sermons but never had it hit home so much for me as it did now. While in the hospital, with my pastor, Pastor Sal, and his wife Dena, standing in the ER with Rich's body, Pastor Sal prayed, "God, we don't want this, and we don't like this, but we *trust You.*" Wow! What a short and yet so profound prayer! It perfectly summed up what I was feeling! The primary feeling was, "No, God, no, You can't do this to me," and the secondary feeling was, "Okay, God, if this is Your plan, I will *trust You* that everything is going to be okay." The raw honesty of "I don't want this!" and the purposing of "Okay, I will trust You anyway" was a powerful combination.

And so that became my daily prayer, my prayer several

times a day, my prayer when I woke up in the morning, and my prayer when I laid my head down at night. "God, I don't want this, and I don't like this, but I trust You." Sometimes it was said through anguished tears, and sometimes it was said through a clenched jaw and steely resolve. Sometimes it was the only thing I said because I simply had no other words to pray.

Romans 8:26 (AMP) says,

> *The Spirit [comes to us and] helps us in our weakness. We do not know what prayer to offer ..., but the Spirit Himself [knowing our need at the right time] intercedes on our behalf with sighs and groanings too deep for words.*

And that is exactly what He did. There were days when I was at a loss for words and did not know what to pray, but I just kept praying this short prayer, and the Holy Spirit used it to intercede with God the Father on my behalf. There were days that I did not even pray this prayer but just looked up to heaven and sobbed, knowing that the Holy Spirit knew my heart, knew what I needed, and went to God on my behalf. I cannot tell you how much this helped me cope and gave me peace, knowing that I did not need to offer up long, wordy, redundant prayers to God but that, even without words, I could directly communicate with Him through the Holy Spirit living inside of me.

Dear believers, I would encourage you to make this your prayer (or something similar) when you are going through a difficult time. First of all, admitting to God that you do not like the situation you are in is a very freeing experience. It lifts the burden of pretense off of your shoulders. God knows your heart anyway, and He knows exactly what you are thinking and feeling. He loves you despite what you may be thinking. He loves you when you are mad at Him, He loves you when you are upset with Him, and He loves you when you are disappointed and do not understand.

Second of all, telling God that you trust Him anyway, no matter what your circumstances are, is a testament to how strong your faith is and how serious you are in your submission to Him and His will. Trust suggests true love and devotion. Trust suggests leaving yourself open and vulnerable, knowing He will not harm or hurt you. Trust suggests that despite what is going on, you know that God already knew this was going to happen, that God will be with you every step of the way, and that God's plan for your future will always be good.

In addition to this, the prayers of others upheld and sustained me, even in my darkest moments. I had so many people praying for me, in the morning, in the evening, and at all times. Do not underestimate the power of prayer! There were times when I could literally feel that I had gotten through my day only because of the prayers being offered up to God on my behalf. There could have been no other way. I would encourage you to consider always being in a spirit of prayer. Ephesians 6:18 says, "Pray in the Spirit at all times and on every occasion. Stay alert and be persistent in your prayers for all believers everywhere."

This does not mean that you spend every day, day in and day out, on your knees praying, that you neglect all avenues of life, work, chores, etc., in order to pray. May I suggest that you consider always being in an "attitude of prayer," that is, always be ready to offer up a quick prayer for someone if the Holy Spirit leads you to do it. Do you ever have one of those days where you have someone on your mind all day, and you don't know why? Could it be the Holy Spirit bringing that person to your mind so that you could pray for them? You may not even know why you should be praying for them, but God knows the reason. If someone pops into your mind, say a quick prayer for them. If you know what they're dealing with, pray specifically for that situation. If you don't know if they are having any problems, pray for them anyway; pray that God will bless them and help them with anything they may be going through. I really cannot emphasize this enough! This is one of the main reasons why I'm still here, why I'm doing as well as I am, because of the prayers of others! James 5:16 says, "The earnest prayer of a righteous person has great power and produces wonderful results."

During this time, I also discovered the verse Psalm 6:2–3, "Have compassion on me, Lord, for I am weak. Heal me, Lord, for my bones are in agony. I am sick at heart. How long, O Lord, until you restore me?" I read this verse many times and made it my prayer. I certainly felt weak, my bones were certainly in agony, and I was certainly sick at heart. I love this heart-felt plea from

David, who wrote this psalm. I love the honesty of it. I love that David was begging God to have compassion on him. I love that David was even questioning how long it would be until God restored him? There is nothing wrong with questioning God. God does not expect us to be robots, to never question, to just blindly obey no matter what may be going on in our hearts and minds.

Dear reader, please always remember to keep your prayers honest; God knows what is in your heart anyway!

CHAPTER 3: APRIL

On April 1st, I posted a meme on my Facebook page that said, "The only way that God can show us He's in control is to put us in situations we can't control." Now I know how true that is! As a Christian, I would be the first person to agree with you that "God was in control," in control of everything, the world, the universe, and yes, I would have even agreed with you that God was in control of my life. But looking back, I wonder if I had really, truly believed it—believed it with my whole heart, mind, and soul.

I can say now that I really and truly believe it. In fact, I know it. And my friend, that is exactly what God did to me. He put me in a situation that I had absolutely no control over, and He did indeed show me that He was in control. He showed me He was in control in so many ways. I can honestly say that I was taken care of in every way possible. I don't know how I did it, I still even look back and wonder how I got through it, but I did. God was with me. God was in control. God protected my children and me at this time. God sent amazing people to me to help take care of things. My brother-in-law and nephew were an especially wonderful blessing at this time. I don't know how I would have gotten through the first couple of weeks without them. I could see the hand of God at work in all the circumstances surrounding me.

I sometimes wonder if a believer can actually fully comprehend how much God is in control until they have been thrown into a situation where they had no control. I almost think that it is impossible to fully comprehend it. You really have to experience it first-hand. In all reality, we are in control of nothing; we really are not. Everything can change in the blink of an eye. Your life can change dramatically in a moment.

A single, dramatic, life-changing event can not only make you realize that God is in control and you are not but can also give you the *peace* of knowing that *God is in control and you are not.*

It was at this time that I fully realized that God knew exactly what my future was going to hold, even though I had no idea.

The problem was that I did not know what my future was going to hold. I still had acute emotional pain. I still missed Rich so much. I still had a hard time reconciling in my mind that he was truly gone. I could not see my future in any way, shape, or form. I could not even look a week ahead in my life. Because of COVID-19, the whole country was shut down, and I was no longer working. April was a long, dark, and bleak month. I kept trying to imagine what my future was like, but it was impossible.

Still, in the back of my mind, I did know that God was in control and that He did love me. But yet, I could see nothing in front of me. It was hard, knowing deep in my heart that God loved me and that He had a plan for me, and yet I felt at times that there was no evidence of it. I could sit and count my blessings, and yet my mind would wander into dark places where the blessings were not enough. And so, I began a long journey of waiting. Waiting and trusting. Trusting God.

It was in April that I discovered Psalm 37:7, "Be still in the presence of the Lord, and wait patiently for him to act." I started to realize that "being still" and "waiting patiently" were not passive acts; they were not something that just happened as I went along, I had to train myself to do it, and I had to practice doing it. It was something that first thing in the morning when I woke up, I had to purpose in my heart that I was going to do it. It was something I had to remind myself to do all day long.

If you are a believer and you are going through a hard time, please know that being a believer does not automatically give you immunity from hard times, nor does it shorten your journey of grief, nor does it give you some kind of magical power to take away emotional pain. If you are going through a hard time, you have to *go through* the hard time. There is no other way around it. You do not get a "get out of jail free" card, so to speak. You have to take it day by day, moment by moment. You have to feel the pain, acknowledge the pain, and give it to *God*.

But I can promise you, I can promise you with every breath of my entire being, that you *will not go through it alone*! God is there! He walks every step with you, sustains you, comforts you, and guides you. Yes, I was going through a very difficult and painful time, but I never felt that for one moment, I was doing it alone. Was it hard? Yes! Did I feel lonely at times? Yes! But God was always there. I had a deep inner peace that could not be explained. I was even surprised at it. I had an inner strength that carried me through every moment, every day. That was the *power of God* in me because it was not by my own strength.

Isaiah 40:29 (AMP) says, "(God) gives strength to the weary, And to him who has no might He increases power." This is so true! I am more than happy to say this again and again: *God is everything He claims to be!* I've not only seen it time after time, but I have lived it. I had no strength, I was broken and tired, and He increased my power. God did it; I did not. Like I've said before, I was actually surprised by the strength I had most days! And it did not go unnoticed by those around me. Little by little, day by day, I got stronger and stronger.

God says in 2 Corinthians 12:9 (AMP) that "(His) power is being perfected [and is completed and shows itself most effectively] in [your] weakness." That is so true! It was in my weakest moments that God's power showed through the most! It was in my darkest moments that His light shined the brightest! It was when I could not go on for one more minute that He lifted me up and gave me strength beyond what I knew I was capable of!

If you truly have accepted Jesus Christ as your Savior, then you have the Holy Spirit in you, and you have that same *inner strength*! You have the strength to do things you never thought you were capable of doing.

If you are reading this and not sure about all of it, then please let me assure you that Jesus is waiting for you! He is waiting for you with open arms! He loves you so much that He died for you, and all He wants is for you to put your trust in Him! This inner strength that I talk about can be yours too! And not only that but true peace, joy, and happiness can be yours as well! And most importantly, you can have *hope*. Hope for a wonderful eternity waiting for you when you die; hope for today and tomorrow, no matter what comes.

By the end of April, I felt I was at some kind of impasse. I was waiting, yet I did not know what I was waiting for. I kept going back to Psalm 37:7, reading it all the time. The shock of Rich's death had worn off. I had accepted that he was gone. I had put my trust entirely in God, and He carried me through my grief. I was waiting on God to heal me, and little by little, He began to put the broken pieces of my heart back together. I do not mean that, by April, I was feeling fine, but God was healing the wounds in my heart, and I was beginning to feel okay. I felt all right. At times I was beginning to feel peace in my heart and soul.

But again, I was waiting, and I did not know what I was waiting for. I was waiting for the Lord to act. Waiting is the hardest part of the journey of grief. Waiting for God to do something in your situation is the hardest part of the journey. It is also the loneliest part of the journey. Waiting is also the strongest test of your faith. I still had my friends and family who were always checking in, always calling, and always texting, but it was a little bit fewer texts and longer in between phone calls. This is the part of the journey where it was just God and me—the creator and His created, the Father and His daughter, the maker and His beloved.

Whether you are a believer or an unbeliever, I just want you to know that whatever you are going through, no matter how difficult it may be or how painful it may be, *your situation is not permanent*! It will not last forever, even if there seems to be no end in sight! Even at my darkest times, when there seemed to be no end, I knew that one year from now, two years from now, even ten years from now, things would be different. I didn't know how they would be different, and I certainly did not know how I would ever laugh and have a happy life again, but I knew it would not be the same as the dark place I was in right now. This was the hope that I clung to when the waiting and waiting seemed to go on forever. I put my trust in God that He would take care of me and everything would be okay, but I had absolutely no idea how that could be entirely possible. But I did know that God loved me, and I did believe that He had a good plan for my life.

Does this make me sound crazy, or that I was "blindly" trusting in God? Yes, I suppose I was "blindly" trusting in

Him. I love Ephesians 3:20 (AMP), which says,

> *Now to Him who is able to [carry out His*
> *purpose and] do superabundantly more than*
> *all that we dare ask or think [infinitely beyond*
> *our greatest prayers, hopes, or dreams],*
> *according to His power that is at work within*
> *us.*

I had, at this point, decided to take God at His word that He would do superabundant things in my life that were greater than my prayers, hopes, or dreams. I could not begin to imagine how that could be possible, but as I said, I decided to take God at His word and believe that He was exactly who He claimed to be.

And so, during my time of waiting, I discovered Psalm 40:1, "I waited patiently for the Lord, and he turned to me and heard my cry."

And then…things started to happen.

.

CHAPTER 4: MAY

As I had said previously, April had been a really bad month for me. Things had started to quiet down. It was actually a relief to me. I enjoyed the peace and quiet. It had rained almost every day that month. I was not working, churches were closed, and even going to the grocery store was weird with everyone wearing masks and staying away from each other.

When it got to the end of the month, I had fallen into a deep depression, and I got very sad and depressed. I did not reach out to anyone; I just bore it alone in solitude. The last week of April, however, brought me some surprises.

A friend had stopped by unannounced with a gift, a homemade quilted pillow with a picture of Rich and the kids sewn into the front of the pillow. She had gotten the picture off of Facebook. It was a complete surprise and absolutely beautiful.

I had also gotten a card in the mail from a friend who I had not seen in quite some time. In it was a long hand-written note about how she was always praying for me, how strong I was, and that I was an inspiration to so many people.

Two other friends stopped by with a card and a gift.

A couple of friends had posted beautiful messages on my Facebook page.

My cellphone *exploded* with encouraging texts from absolutely everyone I knew, and I had so many phone calls that I could not get done with one call before another call came ringing in.

And last but certainly not least, I had stepped outside my house only to discover that a dear friend had quietly stopped by my house and left a bag of thoughtful gifts, flowers, and a card on my doorstep.

This had all happened in the space of one week. It was overwhelming! It brought me so much joy that I couldn't stop crying! How did friends know I needed an encouraging word on my Facebook page? How did a friend think to send me a card three months later? How did a large number of friends wake up one morning during that week and know that they needed to send me a text? How did a friend take the time to put together a bunch of gifts for me and drop them off at my house three months after Rich had died? What made people take time out of their busy schedule to make sure that they called me to see if I was doing okay? There was only one way to describe it, and I put it into words in a post on my Facebook page in May. It said,

"I'm writing this post with tears in my eyes…on

January 29, 2020, I had the most awful thing happen to my children and me. Through all the tears and pain, I've continued to trust God that not only would I see Rich again one day, but that in the meantime, *He* would provide for me, and *He* would give us strength to get through each day and *He* would give us peace in the middle of the storm. Let me assure you that not only has *He* done that, but so much more. *God* is exactly who *He* says *He* is, and I have been experiencing this first-hand. The last two weeks have been especially dark and sad for me as I have been missing Rich so much I can hardly bear it. And the outpouring of love, texts, phone calls, and gifts I have received has been absolutely overwhelming! It's not my birthday or special occasion, nor did I talk to anyone and tell them how much I needed cheering up; this is simply *God* at work! I have amazing, loving, and sensitive friends who, when God speaks to their heart to do something for someone else, they do it!"

Yes, that pretty much sums it up. It was *God*. It was *my God*! It was my Father, my creator, the one who loves me more than anyone else ever has or ever will. God pours out His love over us through the Holy Spirit, but He also shows His love to us through others. And I had felt so much love that week; there are no words to describe it. It was more than overwhelming; it was actually experiencing the presence of the living and true God. It really solidified in my mind, heart, and soul that God really existed and that He was really here with me. It was so solid and steadfast within me that nothing or no one would ever change my mind. It is not only something I believe in but a part of who I am. It is something I would die for. It is something that I need to share with others.

It was at that point that I began to put things in perspective. Rich was gone. I was still here with my son and my daughter. Life would go on, and it was worth living because God was with me, and a God-filled life is a life worth living.

And so, it was in May when I wrote that Facebook post, and it was in May that I started to realize that I was going to be okay because I was in God's hands. And like it says in Romans 8:38–39,

> *And I am convinced that nothing can ever separate us from God's love. Neither death nor life, neither angels nor demons, neither our fears for today nor our worries about tomorrow—not even the powers of hell can separate us from God's love. No power in the sky above or in the earth below—indeed, nothing in all creation will ever be able to separate us from the love of God that is revealed in Christ Jesus our Lord.*

That's right, fellow believer. If you are a child of God, *nothing* will ever separate you from His love. Times may get hard, and you may get sick, but God will never leave you. You may even, in anger, turn your back on God for a time, but again, He will never leave you. You cannot run from Him, and you cannot hide from Him. God's love is so perfect and true that we cannot even fathom it. We cannot explain it because it is so different from how we as humans love. But we can embrace it, believe it, and allow it to flood our souls and fill our lives. This is truly what makes life worth living.

If you are not sure about all of this, please know that this love that I speak of, as described in Romans 8, is available to you as well. You need only to believe it and receive it. And belief, that's the difficult part, right? It is so hard for us to truly realize and accept God's love because it is perfect in its entirety and has nothing to do with us ever doing anything to earn it. Our concept of love is based on the examples of how we have been loved in our lifetimes and how we love others. While we *practice* love and do our best to love fully, we fall short time and time again, but God *is* love. God's love is *love on steroids, love times infinity, love to the moon and back a thousand times over*.

Consider these words from 1 John,

> *Love is from God ...God is love. [He is the originator of love, and it is an enduring attribute of His nature.] ...God has sent His [One and] only begotten Son ...into the world so that we might live through Him. ...(T)his is love, not that we loved God, but that He loved us.*
> **1 John 4:7–10 (AMP)**

God loves you so much and wants you to accept His love and love Him in return. Please realize that God will not love you once you accept Him, but He loves you fully and completely right now! What an amazing thought. Would you possibly consider that today would be the day that you will go to God, accept His love, and become one of His children?

It was also during this time that I received a letter from a woman that I did not know that had attended Waymart Church. She had become a widow approximately one and a half years before I did. She wrote me a most endearing, beautiful letter that had come straight from her heart as one who had already gone through and continued to go through the same journey that I was going through. The letter was detailed and intimate. As soon as I had started the letter, I cried as I had read through it. What an impact it had on me! A sister-in-Christ, who I had never met, had heard of my tragedy, and it truly and deeply affected her, as she knew exactly what I was going through. She had taken the time to hand-write a letter to me and describe her painful circumstances, as well as how God was with her and how He would be with me as well. This was the sympathy card that had meant more to me than any other because it was from someone who *knew what I was going through*. Remember how I had talked about God's love being love on steroids? Well, this was a sympathy card on steroids!

This letter had a two-fold effect on me: first of all, it was the most comforting sympathy card I had received, and it truly gave me the peace as I read about this woman's journey and how God was with her and she was doing okay, that *He would do the same for me*.

Secondly, it made me realize that because of what I was experiencing, I could now be there for others in this way, and my comfort would be true and genuine because I really would know what the other person was feeling as I had been there myself. Second Corinthians 1:3–4 tells us,

> *God is our merciful Father and the source of all comfort. He comforts us in all our troubles so that we can comfort others. When they are troubled, we will be able to give them the same comfort God has given us.*

I knew that this tragedy I had experienced was, in and of itself, not a good thing, but good things could happen through it, and people could be helped and comforted. More important than that, God could be glorified through it. Was I willing to use my tragedy to help others? Yes, I was willing, especially since I had experienced first-hand how the sympathy from someone else who had gone through the same thing greatly affected and comforted me. Could God be glorified through it? I wasn't sure. Could my life now as a widow glorify God? As I pondered that question, it was at this time that I began to contemplate that there was possibly a bigger picture here. There was much more to all of this than I realized. It was not all about *me*. If not me, then who was it all about? God? Jesus Christ? Other people? Believers? Unbelievers? I wasn't sure. But I began to realize that perhaps this whole situation was bigger than me, that it was much more than what I was experiencing at the moment.

May 22nd was my daughter Cheyenne's fourteenth

birthday and also her first birthday without her dad. Because COVID-19 was so new, parties and gatherings seemed to be out of the question. Even if I had been totally comfortable with it, others were not. I had decided to give Cheyenne a "drive-through birthday party" where I had invited friends and relatives to stop by individually to visit Cheyenne outside, at a distance that was comfortable to them. I had set up a schedule of visits spaced a half-hour apart over the course of three days. I was amazed at everyone's willingness and enthusiasm! Cheyenne's three-day party was filled with surprise visitors, gifts, balloons, cookies, banners, and plenty of smiles and love!

Everyone's response was so overwhelming and really warmed my heart. To see my daughter enjoying her birthday and getting attention was exactly what my heart needed to see and experience. It truly was one of the great healing moments of this whole experience. It is one thing to suffer, but it is quite another thing to watch your child suffer. My children's pain eclipsed my own. My heart broke more for them than it ever did for me. I will always remember these three days and all the love everyone showed for Cheyenne and what it meant to me.

Since mid-March, most businesses were closed down as well as churches, and it was two days after Cheyenne's birthday, May 24th, that Waymart Church opened back up. What a joyful time that was for me, even though it was a bit surreal with masks, social distancing, and hand sanitizer. To be with my church family again was what I needed more than I realized. I had no idea how starved

I was for their love, to see their faces, and to be able to talk to them in person. It was at this time that I realized how much of a people-person I really was, how much I needed to be around other people, to love them, and to feel their love for me. This realization put me back to the previous thoughts I had about there being a bigger picture here. I started to really feel the pull to help others, love others, and show them the love of God. But I still did not know how that could tie into my current situation. I was still shell-shocked, still hurting, but I could feel the beginnings of a desire on my part to live my life for others and for God.

The first Sunday church was open; I was there with my children, sitting towards the back. When the service was over, I turned around to see who was sitting behind me. Two rows back (because of social distancing) was a whole row of people, but I only saw one person. He was tall, dark-haired, and dark-eyed. I immediately knew who he was. He was Bob, and I had recognized him as the bassist on our church's worship team. Our eyes met for a moment; I smiled at him, which he could not see because I was wearing a mask, and then I turned back around. I did not see anyone else there in that row on that Sunday morning, just Bob. Everyone else was a blur, but he stood out. I had glanced at everyone behind me but made eye contact with him.

The month of May was somewhat of the beginning of a change for me. There was an imperceptible shift in my heart. I had gone from despair to a shred of hope. I felt like I was in a dark tunnel but had seen a tiny glimmer of light. I had gone from experiencing the great comfort of God to experiencing the beginnings of His great love for me. I had gone from believing in God to beginning to really experience a relationship with Him. There was great hurt and sorrow in me, and at the same time, the expectation of something good coming my way. There was the sadness of the ending of a life and the exciting beginning of a new life lived in a completely different way. Two polar opposite sets of emotions living inside of me at the same time. It was disconcerting and intoxicating at the same time.

CHAPTER 5: JUNE

The book of Ecclesiastes, chapter 3, verses 1 through 8, describes the different seasons in life that we all experience. Verse one says that there is a season for everything and a time for every activity. It talks about a time to be born and a time to die, a time to plant and a time to harvest. I would like to focus on verse four, which says, "[There is a] time to cry and a time to laugh. A time to grieve and a time to dance." At this point in my journey, this is what I was experiencing, and experiencing it in different ways.

First of all, I was experiencing a time to cry and a time to laugh, and sometimes it was all on the same day. I have to admit that, in the previous months, I had days when I was profoundly sad, but I had other days when I was happy. But I had counted on never again having a day where I would laugh out loud. I had prematurely assumed that, and, looking back, I wonder why I would even have thought such a thing. Especially since I had a relationship with Jesus Christ and knew what kind of joy that can bring. As much as I loved God and knew He loved me, I had just assumed that I would go on with a life that was devoid of laughter. Isn't that crazy? Why would I think that? Why would I believe in a God who promises in His Word that He would give us great joy beyond anything we could imagine but not think I would ever experience that joy? Would He even be a god worth worshipping and following? Obviously, I was basing my opinion on what I was *feeling* instead of focusing on who God is! I was so limited in my human thoughts and feelings that I wasn't grasping the supernatural *power* of who God is and what He can do!

But June was the month when I began to laugh again. I don't remember the specifics; it could have been a line from a movie, something I read, or maybe even something one of my children had said to me, but I laughed. And in the beginning, I felt guilty for laughing. How could I laugh when my husband was dead? But then I had to consider what Rich was experiencing in heaven with Jesus! His body may be lying in the grave, but he is alive and well and in the presence of his Savior and experiencing more than we could ever even begin to comprehend while here on Earth! I had to realize that there was no reason to feel guilty for being happy and laughing and that laughter is a gift from God. And I also knew that Rich would want Dale, Cheyenne, and me to laugh and be happy, not to live out the rest of our life here on Earth sad and grieving.

Second of all, in reading those verses in Ecclesiastes, I have been able to fully understand that, in life, there is a time to be happy and a time to mourn, and no one is exempt from this. I have been able to fully comprehend that this is what God says, and it is true for everyone. In all of our journeys, there are happy times and sad times, and that is the way it is supposed to be. In the happy times, we need to fully embrace and enjoy those times and thank God for them. In the sad times, we need to hold each other close and stay close to God and trust Him to walk with us through it. And I realize that no stage of life is permanent, and I pray, dear reader, that you understand it too. Nothing in life is permanent, and nothing you are going through is permanent even though it may seem to be. Whatever difficulty you are dealing with, it will not be forever, and...our lives are not filled with unending good times and happiness either.

Being able to understand and keep this perspective can help you get through the rough times (knowing it will not be forever) and truly enjoy the good times (knowing the good times do not last forever either). The only thing that does last forever is the eternity that occurs once we die. The choices we make here while living on Earth determine where and what our eternity will be.

And so, in my journey, I was experiencing a time to cry and a time to laugh, and as time went on, there began to be fewer crying times and more laughing times. And as I continued through this, I was reminded of the verse in the book of Jeremiah that says, "If you look for me [God] wholeheartedly, you will find me" (Jeremiah 29:13). And that is what I was doing, looking for God. "Now, wait a minute," you may say. "I thought you already knew God and believed?" Yes, I did, but I continued to look for Him and seek Him out through reading the Bible and praying. I kept wanting to know Him more. I wanted a closer relationship with Him. Hebrews 11:6 (AMP) says, "Whoever comes [near] to God must [necessarily] believe that God exists and that He rewards those who [earnestly and diligently] seek Him." I kept reading that verse believing that God was going to "reward" me for earnestly and diligently seeking Him. And He did exactly that. He rewarded me with an even closer and more intimate relationship with Him. He revealed more about Himself to me through His Word and the Holy Spirit. I begin to love God and Jesus more and more and with my whole heart. And I began to understand truly just how much my heavenly Father God and Savior Jesus Christ loved me. And even as I sit and write this, I still have not been able to fully comprehend the love God has for me! It is more than my human brain can figure out and more than my heart could imagine!

If you are not sure what you believe or if you are not sure if you have a relationship with God, I would encourage you to consider the verse I just mentioned above from Jeremiah. God does and *will* reward anyone who seeks Him wholeheartedly. This applies to believers and skeptics alike. Acts 17:27 says, "His purpose was for the nations to seek after (him) and perhaps feel their way toward him and find him—though he is not far from any one of us." Did you see that last part? God is not far from any one of us! He is not some unreachable foreign entity far away in the heavens. He is close! He is waiting! He has so much love to give you if you are willing to receive it! And check this out—Psalm 14:2 says, "The Lord looks down from heaven on the entire human race; he looks to see ...if anyone seeks God." God is watching everyone looking for anyone that is seeking Him out! That means you! That's right; God is looking for you!

I want you to know right now that God is close, He is looking for you, and He reveals Himself to those who are looking for Him. I would like to encourage you to make this your prayer: "God, I'm not sure if I believe, but I am looking for You. Please reveal Yourself to me." I know He will make Himself known to you; I don't know when and I don't know how, but I know you will have an encounter with God, and it will change your life forever!

If you are a believer, I encourage you to not ever become complacent in your relationship with God and to always be seeking Him out. Look for Him *wholeheartedly* and believe that He is a rewarder of them who *diligently seek Him*! Just as it takes time to get to know someone, it takes time to develop a relationship with God. He is always there waiting for us, and we need to be going to Him, continuously going to Him. James 4:8 says, "Come close to God, and God will come close to you," and again, in Acts 17:27 it says, "[God's] purpose was for the nations to seek after God and perhaps feel their way toward him and find him—though he is not far from any one of us." Isn't that wonderful that God is not far from any one of us, and He is always there waiting with open arms?

And so, the month of June was a pivotal point in my journey. I had the unexpected pleasure of taking my relationship with God to the next level. As I was searching for Him and reaching for Him, I found Him! I already knew God but now knew Him on a more intimate level. This filled me with so much joy! This helped to heal my heart in a way that can't be explained. It did not make my loss any less great than it was, but it made me rest in God's love and let Him hold me and take care of me. Remember back when I talked about my early prayer of, "God, reveal Yourself to me in a mighty way" and how that had started a tiny ember glowing in my soul? Well, the ember began to grow bigger and burn stronger.

It was also in the month of June that I stumbled on the name "Bob Wilson" on social media. I recognized him as the man I had seen in church, the bassist on our worship team, one of the souls that had ventured out to church when we first re-opened amidst the COVID-19 epidemic, and the man I had locked eyes with over masks that same Sunday. I noticed that not only did he play bass on our worship team, but he was also a jazz musician.

That detail must have stuck in my mind because as I was watching an old movie one Friday night about a jazz club, I thought to myself, *I bet that Bob Wilson guy would like this*. I contacted him online about it, which started a brief conversation between us. Little could I have imagined what that short conversation was about to start...

CHAPTER 6: JULY

The month of July was very hot, hotter than it had been in the last couple of years. I was able to keep myself busy with growing my flowers, gardening, and swimming. Summer is my favorite season, and I really began to relax and enjoy it, although it was weird going through summer without Rich.

I was reading my Bible and praying more than ever, and the peace I felt in my heart could not be explained. It was supernatural. I was also spending more time in my church, serving wherever I could. I prayed every morning for God to show me where I could serve Him that day and who I could help. I called and texted people whom God had laid on my heart to encourage. I begin to think again about the verse in Jeremiah that I knew so well, "'For I know the plans I have for you,' says the Lord. 'They are plans for good …, to give you a future'" (Jeremiah 29:11). I began to wonder if God had other plans for me, and if so, what could they be? Was there a bigger picture here than just me helping out in my church?

I remember floating in my pool on many a day thinking about all of this. I remember that the sun felt so hot on my skin and that it felt like the warmth of God on me. I felt as though the Holy Spirit was trying to communicate with me, but I couldn't understand. I felt such a burden to help others, especially the hurting. And I knew it wasn't just helping those who were hurting from a loss; it was helping anyone who was hurting in any way. I wanted people to understand that there was hope amidst the pain, that there was so much love and peace and healing with God.

Psalm 25:1, 4–5 became my prayer, "O Lord, I give my life to you. …Show me the right path, O Lord; point out the road for me to follow. Lead me by your truth and teach me." Now, remember, God is a rewarder of them "who [earnestly and diligently] seek Him" (Hebrews 11:6, AMP), and He began to speak to my heart.

My first impulse is to tell you that I got this crazy idea to do a ladies' Bible study at my house. And why would it have been a crazy idea? Because I was not a public speaker. I was not a teacher. I could not talk in front of people, even a small group of people. Even having to introduce myself at one of our small group Bible studies at the church was enough to give me an anxiety attack. The truth is it wasn't my crazy idea, it was God's idea, and He revealed to me that He wanted me to start a Bible study in my home. It didn't seem to matter to God that I was not a public speaker, it did not matter to God that I was not a teacher, and it did not matter to God that I couldn't even introduce myself at a small group Bible study. God wanted me to do it, and He meant it.

When I say God "spoke" to me, I don't mean that I heard a voice from heaven; it was through the Holy Spirit that He spoke to me. It was a very strong feeling I had in my soul, and I knew it was from God and not my own thoughts. It was undeniable, although the thought of it was intimidating. I began to think about how I could put this plan into action and realized I was saying "yes" to what God was asking me. Once I said yes, ideas came very quickly! I knew that I was going to invite some close friends to the Bible study, friends that I was very comfortable with. Their names came quickly to my mind. I asked God, "What could my study be about?" and He answered, "Talk to these ladies about fear." And it was perfect because we were right in the middle of the COVID-19 epidemic, and there was still so much fear and uncertainty flowing around. I felt as though this also went along with my desire to help those who were hurting because so many were suffering from fear of the pandemic and the unknown going on in the world as well.

I got very excited as I pulled out a notebook and started writing notes and looking up Bible verses. And so my first Bible study began! It was a five-week study with five lessons. I was so excited! I invited five close friends and my mom, and everyone said yes.

I was so excited about this new adventure God was leading me on!

But then, the day of the first study actually came, and

all the excitement melted away. It was replaced with intimidation, worry, and fear. Funny, isn't it, that I was fearful of doing a Bible study on fear. Who says God doesn't have a sense of humor? Before everyone arrived, I started getting nauseous. I begin to seriously doubt myself and doubt God. Once everyone was at the house, and I began the study and started to talk, my hands and voice were visibly shaking. My hands continued to shake the whole time. I kept losing my place and my train of thought and would have to sit there quietly for a minute or two with my face red with embarrassment as I collected my thoughts and found my place again. Somehow I managed to muddle through it. My six wonderful ladies were so patient and kind and encouraging to me! And they all came back again the next week!

Throughout the week, I thought about the Bible study and about how I was not the teacher that I had dreamed I would be. God brought to my attention the Bible verse that I had repeatedly gone to in April; "'My grace is all you need. My power works best in weakness.' So now I am glad to boast about my weaknesses, so that the power of Christ can work through me" (2 Corinthians 12:9). I realized that God led me to do something I was not good at so He could show me how His power could shine through me if I would allow Him to. I realized that there was no limit to what I could do for God. If He wanted me to do it, then He would give me everything I would need to accomplish it!

I also realized that I needed to let go of trying to control the study myself and trust Him to be in control and to give me the words to say. I begin to pray, "Your words, God, not mine," every week before the study. I began to feel God speaking through me, and what an amazing feeling it was! It was exhilarating! I can hardly describe it; yes, it was my words and my voice speaking, and yet everything was composed by God.

Dear believer, have you ever said "yes" to God? Has He ever impressed upon your heart to do something for Him? And I don't mean just speaking or doing a Bible study. I mean anything; helping in Sunday school, cooking dinner for someone, cleaning your church building, sending someone a card, visiting someone who is home-bound. The list is endless. God needs His children everywhere doing all kinds of things for Him. Has He ever asked you to do something, and you've said to yourself, "I'll do that when I have more time," or "I can't do that," or just flat-out ignored the request? I'd like to encourage you to be sensitive to what God may be asking of you. Say yes to God! I have found that the deepest joy I have ever experienced has been when I have been right in the middle of God's will, doing exactly what He has asked me to do. There's no feeling like it.

If you think God is asking you to do something that you are not good at, go ahead and try it. If what you are trying is really what He wants for you, you'd be surprised at what you can do! God will supply you with everything you need. God is so awesome that way! You may also find that what you are trying may not be exactly the right fit for you, which may lead you in another direction. And that's okay too! Keep trying, and don't give up.

If you are reading this and not sure if you believe or how much of it you believe, this may seem very foreign to you. For years, I have had the feeling of not quite belonging wherever I was. Have you ever had that feeling? When I said yes to having a deeper relationship with God and starting living my life in tune with Him and whatever He had for me, I really started to feel a sense of belonging. I knew I had a purpose, and I knew my life had meaning. It was a very peaceful feeling. If you have a feeling of not quite belonging anywhere, might I suggest that it may be because you are not in the family of God yet? Maybe God is asking you to be part of His family right now, and you don't quite know what to say. This I know for sure; He loves you, and He wants you! If you go to Him and say "yes," He will take you right now, exactly the way you are! I would encourage you to not wait another day or even another minute going to God and telling Him that you want to be part of His family!

If you're still hesitant, that's okay too! Want to know why? Because God wants you to come to Him when you are ready. God does not force people to believe in Him. He waits with open arms. He sends His Holy Spirit to come to you and love on you and help you. If you are still trying to figure this all out, don't give up! Keep looking! Remember, God says that He is a "rewarder of them who diligently seek Him." Keep asking God to reveal Himself to you.

As each week went on, I became more relaxed in my Bible study. I actually began to enjoy myself. The best part of it all was that as I was studying God's Word to prepare for each lesson, I was getting to know God more!

In the meantime, the online messages between Bob Wilson and me became more frequent. I had discovered that he was a painter, and so the majority of his work during the summer was spent outside. As I had mentioned before, it was an exceptionally hot July that year. We frequently talked about the brutal summer and him being out in it working. He described his different jobs to me, and I would tell him about my work as well. We talked about how we both loved to swim and to be outside in nature. We began to get to know each other a little more.

I soon found myself waking up each hot morning thinking of Bob and whatever job he was on that day. I would pray, "God, please protect my friend Bob from the heat today." I would message him some mornings and tell him that I was praying for him and for him to be safe in the heat that day. He would message back and tell me he was praying that I would have a good day too. It's always so nice to know when a friend is praying for you!

Sometimes we would message each other in the evening as well and talk about how our days went. As time went on, I realized I was waiting for those messages. It made me feel as if I had ended my day on a good note.

I saw Bob every Sunday in church. Our greetings were always very friendly but slightly hesitant at first. We became quite comfortable with each other quickly, however, and I began to go up to the stage after the church service and wait for him while he packed his bass away. He was very open and friendly, and I enjoyed talking to him. Like me, he had some unconventional interests and so it was nice to have someone to share with. I began to look forward to our after-church conversations every week, and I was to find out later that he looked forward to them as well.

July was a month of an unexpected revelation to me. As I got to know God more intimately and His great love for me, I wanted to serve Him more. I prayed earnestly for Him to show me what He wanted me to do but did not expect that He would want me to do a Bible study. Out of all the things that I thought about that I *could* do for God, it did not occur to me that He would want me to do something that I *could not* do without His help.

At the beginning of the year, I found that I had to step out in faith and trust God that He would take care of me and that I would be okay. I now had to step out in faith again and trust God that He would take care of me and that I would be able to do what He was asking me to do. Stepping out in faith (not knowing what is going to happen) is a hard thing to do, but seeing how God had carried me so far in the year gave me the courage to step out in faith and do my Bible study. Being obedient to God in this brought me many unexpected blessings. First of all, studying God's Word enriched my life and my relationship with God beyond compare. Second, I have had the privilege of getting to know my friends that came to my Bible study on a deeper level and been able to watch friendships grow between them as well. Last of all, it gave me confidence in who I was as a child of God and what I was capable of doing when I trusted in Him.

CHAPTER 7: AUGUST

My life took a completely unexpected turn in August. It was something that I never saw coming, and I can't stress this enough; I did *not* see it coming! It was shocking, scary, exciting, and euphoric all at the same time. But more of that later!

First, I would like to share some Bible verses with you that I discovered in the month of August that really spoke to me and perfectly described my situation. The first one is Psalm 27:13; "Yet I am confident I will see the Lord's goodness while I am here in the land of the living." As a believer, I know that whatever hardships I am experiencing here while living on Earth are "nothing compared to the glory that (God) will reveal to us later" (Romans 8:18). In other words, it will all be okay in the end. No matter how hard life may get, I know that my life will pass, and eventually, I will be with my Savior, Jesus Christ.

However, this verse in Psalms reminded me that I will see the Lord's goodness while still living here in this life on Earth as well! Life is not all about suffering and then receiving a great reward in the end. There is joy and peace and happy times with God in the here and now as well. This joy, peace, and happiness are not dictated by what our circumstances are; it is dependent on what is going on inside of our hearts. I was, at that time, experiencing the goodness of the Lord! I was experiencing joy and peace that I had not felt since Rich died and actually had not felt in many years before that. God says that the peace He gives "exceeds anything we can understand" (Philippians 4:7). It's so true! And there were times when I was so joyful I had a difficult time reconciling the joy and peace I was feeling inside, considering the fact that I was a widow of seven months at that time.

I continued on with my home Bible study and serving in my church. I was still waking up every morning and asking God to show me what I could do for Him and who I could help that day, but now I was doing it with excitement and anticipation of what was in store for me that day! I was waking up every morning with a hopeful feeling instead of a hopeless feeling.

The other verse was 1 Peter 5:10b, "After you have suffered a little while, he will restore, support, and strengthen you, and he will place you on a firm foundation." In my pain, God had supported me and given me strength. He placed me on a firm foundation. That firm foundation was the truth of who God is and who I was as His child. It was the truth of the fact that He is in control and that "God causes everything to work together for the good of those who love God and are called according to his purpose for them" (Romans 8:28). It was also the truth that,

> *Nothing can ever separate us from God's love. (Not) death nor life, neither angels nor demons, neither our fears for today nor our worries about tomorrow—not even the powers of hell can separate us from God's love.*

Romans 8:38

The best part of all was that God restored me. The word "restore" means to bring back or return something to a former condition, place, or position. I don't know how He did it, but God took the broken me and returned me back to the whole person I was before all of this happened. Not only did He return me back to who I was, but I was a better person, more aware of how precarious life can be and that we need to make each day count, and we need to love and live life with abandon! We need to be there for each other and help each other, and that is why we are here! Months ago, I could not even imagine how I could have been happy again, and yet, I was. I was very happy. It had nothing to do with me and had everything to do with God, how amazing He is, and how amazing my relationship with Him was. People I had come in contact with said that I was "glowing" or that I had a "glow about me."

That "glow" was not a result of any kind of happiness or enlightenment that I had attained. One very insightful friend had put it this way, "I can see the Holy Spirit bubbling out of you." That "glow" that others were seeing was the joy of Jesus Christ in me. I was "in love" with Jesus! I was excited about knowing Him and His love for me and sharing that love with others! This is not something that happened overnight. It was many months of searching, praying, and tears. It was months of asking "why." It was months of saying, "I just don't understand." And it was months of asking God to "please reveal Yourself to me in a mighty way."

And this was where I was. I had weathered the storm and survived. I was content, and I was happy. And I was so very thankful to God and all He had done for me. I had a drive, and I had a purpose, and my purpose was to help the hurting and to point them to Jesus and the love, joy, and peace they can receive through Him. This is my own unique journey and my own unique timeline, and I pray that no one will read this thinking that this is exactly what their experience is supposed to be. Grief is a very personal thing, and everyone does it in different ways and for different periods of time. There are different stages of grief that most experience, but they do it in their own way and in their own time, and it can be anywhere from a couple of months to many years. And there is no right or wrong way of doing it. The time it takes does not directly correspond to how "spiritual" you are or how "deep your relationship with God is." There are many more factors involved than that. It has been my desire from the beginning of this book to share what I (and I alone) was feeling and hope that people could relate to my story in different ways and find hope. Most importantly, that they could find hope in Jesus Christ.

Like I had said previously, this was where I was at, and I was content and happy. It was at that point that my life had taken a completely unexpected turn, and it was something that I never saw coming.

My friendship with Bob continued, and as we got to know each other better, we settled into a comfortable and genuine friendship. After some failed attempts to have an after-church service lunch, I put out the offer for him to come over and have pizza with me one Saturday night. I was so excited as the evening arrived! First of all, it was nice to have some company over on a Saturday night (especially since the whole world was still shut down due to COVID-19, and there was literally nowhere to go and nothing to do). And secondly, since most of our conversations were online or for only ten minutes after a church service, it would be nice to be able to just sit and talk face to face with no time restraints. From what I had gathered so far about Bob, he was unique and quirky in the same way that I was. We had similar interests, and we were both "old souls" that seemed to look at the world differently than most. He also seemed to be a very steadfast and godly man. I was anticipating that we would become very good friends, and because of our unconventional interests, we would be able to do fun things together that I was unable to do with other friends.

Since we had only seen each other in our church setting, it was a little weird and different to be together and talk at my home. It was a beautiful August evening as we sat outside and had pizza together. When he prayed over the food before we ate, something stirred in my soul. His words and the way he prayed greatly encouraged me. Our conversation during dinner was light, but after we ate, we got up and walked around and got into a deeper conversation. One of the great passions of my life is books, and I discovered on that evening that it was a great love of Bob's as well. We talked about the books we were reading (we both read more than one book at the same time), and then our conversation turned to a very lively talk about the Bible. Bob was just as excited as I was about reading God's Word and learning more about Him. Out in public, Bob is quiet and reserved, but I found that one-on-one, he was very open and a great conversationalist. The evening seemed to fly by as we continued to talk about the Bible, different books of the Bible, and verses that were meaningful to us. We talked about where we both were at in our own personal devotions. We both had a similar thirst for God's Word and to soak up as much as we could out of it.

The book of Matthew, chapter 18 and verse 20 says, "Where two or three gather together as my followers, I am there among them." And that evening, I could feel God there with us! I don't know how to explain it, but it was not just Bob and me together; it was as though there was a third person there with us. And it was not just any person; it was the creator of the universe, the one who created both Bob and me and loved us very much. When

Bob left, I felt such a warmth in my heart, and I was so thankful to God for bringing me a new friend. I felt such a desire to see him again, to spend time with him and talk and laugh and enjoy the gift of our friendship. I truly felt that God had brought him especially to be my friend and encouragement in my life.

In my eagerness, I invited him over again the following weekend, and he accepted. This time our conversation became even deeper, and he stayed even longer. One of the things that we discovered was that we were both big *Star Wars* fans and that it was a huge part of both of our childhoods. Our favorite *Star Wars* movie was even the same: *The Empire Strikes Back.* We also shared an interest in the book of Revelation, the last book of the Bible. We decided to do a study together on the book of Revelation that we found online. We found out that the study was seventeen lessons but decided to do it anyway, joking that "if we do one every weekend, we will be done with it in January." For some reason, thinking about seeing Bob consistently every weekend for the next four months made me happy, and I was intrigued that he was just as willing to see me every weekend for the next four months as well.

Bob left late that evening, and the following morning, I went to church and experienced something very startling and confusing. I walked into the sanctuary to find a seat, but as I walked in, I looked up at the stage and saw Bob up there with the rest of the worship team. His head was down, and he was in the middle of doing something, so he did not see me, but I saw him. At that moment, I felt a physical sensation in my chest, as though I had been hit with something and thrown off balance. My heart started pounding, and this explosion of exhilaration washed over me. I knew right at that moment that I was falling for Bob and falling for him hard.

I sat down and tried to compose myself. This did not make sense at all. What was going on? I had only been a widow for seven months now. I had only spent two evenings with this man. I was only beginning to get to know him. We were friends; we had gotten together on the basis of friendship and not with any romantic inclinations. No one falls in love with someone after spending two evenings with them. What I was feeling seemed completely ridiculous to me, so I immediately pushed those feelings to the back of my mind. I refused to entertain it in any way, and I pretended it had not even happened. I told myself that Bob and I were friends, and that was it, end of the story.

The following weekend we dove into our Revelation study on Friday night, and that Sunday, we decided to go to the movies to see a replaying of the classic, *Jaws*. It was the first time we were actually going out in public somewhere. Bob stopped by the house to pick me up, and as I got into his van, I had butterflies in my stomach, and I felt like I was a teenager on my first date. Up until this time, Bob had been coming over to my house, and we were spending time together as friends, having good conversations, and enjoying each other's company. Somehow today felt different. After months of being on lockdown due to COVID-19 and not being able to go anywhere or do anything, it was exhilarating to actually be going out! I was ecstatic! The weather was hot, we were driving with the windows down, and all of a sudden, the world felt open with possibilities. I felt free. Driving to the movie theater, I didn't feel like I was with my "friend" Bob. I now felt like I was with a "date," a man I was interested in, someone I was really beginning to like. Those romantic feelings from last week that I had pushed away were now making a comeback. I felt as though I was being torn in two; only seven months ago, I had buried my husband, and now I was on a date with someone who was making me feel giddy and young again. He was someone I was starting to have strong feelings for. How could this possibly be?

And in the same way that He was there with us when we hung out at my house, God was with us on our first "date" as well. I could feel His presence with us the whole time. So much of our conversations had centered around God and His Word. Even as we were getting to know each other, our interests and our life experiences, our individual relationships with God were always a part of the conversation as well. It was always so natural, always including God in everything we said and did. So, it was only going to be natural that He was with us now as well.

And so, on that Sunday, as I was out on my first actual "date" with Bob, I had peace in my heart. The loss of Rich and the excitement of a possible new love somehow were able to co-exist together inside of me. The old and the new, the tragedy and the joy, the what was and the what now could possibly be. Because of our mutual love of movies old and new, and *Jaws*, in particular, it was safe to say that our first date was a success. We had dinner afterward, and it was the first time that our conversation got a little more personal, open, and vulnerable.

I thought about Bob constantly throughout the following week, and he came over again on Friday. Pizza and Bible study was our weekly routine now, and we both rearranged our schedules as best as we could to accommodate at least one day out of the weekend to do it. My head was telling me that one day out of the week was enough to hang out with a "friend," and yet, my heart was telling me that I wanted to see him much more than that. I was caught in between my thoughts and emotions, and as I pondered it all, I had to laugh at myself a little because I had no idea if Bob even liked me in "that way" or not. I decided to relax, enjoy our time together, and let it go in whatever direction it was going to go in. I decided not to push it in one way or another and just wait and see.

That "decision," however, went right out the window when Bob and I were saying our goodbyes that night. As our evening ended, we did what we usually did; we discussed our plans for the following weekend to see what day we were both free to meet. I couldn't wait any longer and had to make my feelings known, so I said, "Bob, I'm not good at playing games, and so I just have to tell you that I am available to get together with you *anytime* you want because I *really* enjoy spending time with you and I *really*, *really* like you."

And there, it was said, it was out there, and I couldn't take it back.

It was only a moment before Bob responded, and yet it felt like an awkward eternity to me. His response was, "Well, I have to ask you a question first. What do the kids think about me coming over?" I was surprised at that question and yet touched that he was concerned about Dale and Cheyenne's feelings before even telling me what his reaction was. I replied that, as far as I could tell, they were fine with their mom having a friend come over every weekend. They had even spent one evening with us, roasting hot dogs over a bonfire.

He then replied that he felt the same way that I did, and all of a sudden, my whole world turned upside down. I couldn't believe it. I was choked with emotion and started to cry. I was beyond thrilled that he liked me too. I was amazed that after all the pain I had been through, I was still optimistic and open to the excitement of a new romance. I was confused because I wondered how it could possibly be; after all, it had only been seven months since Rich died. I was a little scared, too; I had never been in a situation like this before. I had never been a widow before, never mind a widow who was dating. I had no idea what to expect and how to act in a situation like this. I wondered what people would think. And yet I didn't care what people thought. I knew what I had found in Bob, what a wonderful man he was, and how perfect he was for me in every way. I confessed this all to him, and he agreed because he had never dated a widow, and this was all new to him too.

We both kept repeating the phrase, "I didn't see this coming." We were both completely taken by surprise. I cannot emphasize this enough. We were both shocked by our feelings for each other. Our friendship started out because we had so many of the same interests. There was no hidden agenda on either side. I was a widow who was looking for friendship, not another relationship. Bob was looking for a friend but had no thoughts of jumping into a relationship with a woman who had only been widowed for seven months. We were both lonely and reaching out for companionship, but all of a sudden, it seemed as if something huge was about to happen. Something that was going to change the course of our lives forever.

We decided that we would take our time and pray about our situation. We were determined to be sure that we had God's blessing on our new relationship and that what we were feeling was indeed real. There were Dale and Cheyenne's feelings to consider as well. We decided to move forward and proceed with caution.

And so, we ended the evening happy and excited, and a little nervous too. But one thing was for sure, we were both beginning to have serious feelings for each other, and we were ready to start a new journey together.

CHAPTER 8: SEPTEMBER

The decision that Bob and I made to take our time and proceed forward into our new relationship with caution was completely forgotten within the next couple of weeks. The following Friday night, we shared our first kiss, which was powerful, moving, and so exciting it was like nothing either one of us had experienced before.

The following Friday, five weeks after our first meeting together and two and a half weeks after our first official date, we told each other, "I love you." So much for "taking it slow," right? And yet, it was true. I did love him. And he loved me too. After the night when we both admitted that we had feelings for each other, I prayed non-stop about our situation. I prayed for God's will to be done in our lives. I prayed that we were making the right decision and that our relationship was what God had for us. Bob was praying the same thing as well. And the harder I prayed for clarity in the situation, the deeper I fell in love. I kept asking God, "Is this right? Is this okay?" And the answer I kept getting back was deep peace in my soul, a smile on my face, and inexpressible joy in my heart.

And just as my relationship with Bob progressed, my relationship with God progressed as well. I strived to put God first in my life, and I experienced that putting Him first put all my other relationships into proper perspective. I loved better, stronger, and unconditionally. I was starting to look at people through the eyes of Jesus. Putting God first in my life really made life worth living!

And as I was getting caught up in all the excitement of our new romance, I started to think about the verse in the book of Exodus that says, "For the Lord ...is a God who is jealous about his relationship with you" (Exodus 34:14). The fact that God could be jealous of my new relationship if I put it ahead of Him was a scary thought! I took it seriously. I didn't want Bob to come between God and me. I also knew that if I continued to put God first that my relationship with Bob would thrive as a result, especially if it was what God wanted for me.

At this point, I was also absolutely crazy over Bob. I knew my heart and how fully I loved. I knew that things could get out of control very quickly, and I could lose perspective. I remembered the words that Jesus said in the book of Matthew, "You must love the Lord ...with all your heart, all your soul, and all your mind" (Matthew 22:37). Jesus also said, "Seek the kingdom of God above all else ..., and he will give you everything you need" (Matthew 6:33). I knew that I had to love God and put Him first in my life and seek His "kingdom" (the things which have eternal value) before anything else, and as a result of that, all else would fall into proper place, including my new relationship.

I began to pray to God that, if Bob was going to come between Him and me, He would remove him from my life. I prayed that either he would be removed by me losing interest or by Bob losing interest in me. Believe me, it was not an easy prayer to say! I was completely enamored of Bob and thought about him all the time. I wanted to spend as much time with him as possible. Even as I was saying the words, "God, if Bob comes in between You and me, please take him away," my heart was crying, "Please, no! I don't want to lose him!" But if I had learned anything these last eight months, it was that putting God first in all things and having a close, intimate relationship with Him was the only way to live life! It was the only way to have true joy and peace, and that joy and peace that "passes all human understanding" could not be attained in any other way or relationship.

I would like to encourage you, reader, that as you are reading my words, you think about your own relationship with God. Is there anything or anyone that you put ahead of your relationship with God? I have found myself that it is a very easy thing to do. It is very easy to start putting more time and energy towards something than towards God. In fact, it is something I have to be conscious of daily. Remember that in the book of Exodus that God says He is jealous about your relationship with Him. I ask that you really consider this and do not take it lightly! Jesus says for us to love God with all of our heart, soul, and mind and to seek eternal things above all else, and God will give us what we need.

And not only will He give us what we need! He is willing to bless us with what we want as well! Psalm 37:4 says, "Take delight in the Lord, and he will give you your heart's desires." Wow! If we put God first, He will not only provide us with what we need but will also give us our desires as well, providing that it is what is good for us and coincides with His will for our lives.

I want you to know that God wants you to live a happy life! And remember what I said previously, that true happiness comes from within and not from what is going on all around us. You can be a truly happy and peace-filled person no matter what your circumstances are. Because that true joy within comes from an intimate and fulfilling relationship with God that always comes first. I am not saying this because it is something that I read somewhere, or it is something that I think may happen; I am saying this because I have lived it. Putting God first in all things involves self-sacrifice and self-discipline. It is not easy to do because it goes against the grain of who we are as humans. But I can assure you from personal experience that the benefits far outweigh the work you put in. The benefits will blow your mind! You can live a life that is beyond anything you could have ever hoped for yourself. Always remember that God said, "No mind has imagined what God has prepared for those who love him" (1 Corinthians 2:9).

I do not put out this advice lightly because I know

that praying for God to remove something or someone from your life if it will come between you and Him is a scary thing to do. I prayed it myself and was worried that I would lose Bob. But I knew deep in my soul that it was what I had to do. I meditated on the verse in Proverbs that said, "Seek his will in all you do, and he will show you which path to take" (Proverbs 3:6). I daily asked God to show me which path to take, not only in my life in general but specifically in my relationship with Bob. And guess what God did? He answered me. He gave me my heart's desire. He gave me Bob. He gave me full-blown, out-of-this-world, mind-blowing true love. It seemed impossible, and yet it was true. Looking back now, it seems so easy to see that Bob was God's plan for me, but I didn't know it at the time.

September was the month where God gave me the "go ahead," so to speak, in my relationship with Bob. I had been hesitantly stepping into a relationship with him but could now "free fall" into love with him, and I was enjoying every moment of it! It was a wild ride! And September ended on a very good note. Remember when I said back in August that Bob and I had discovered that we were both huge *Star Wars* fans and that our favorite *Star Wars* movie was the same one? Well, our local theater was showing *The Empire Strikes Back* on the big screen, and we were able to go and see it together. It seemed, in our odd and unconventional way, to be an appropriate way to seal our relationship.

CHAPTER 9: OCTOBER

In the month of October, I once again found myself stepping out of my comfort zone and trusting God with what He wanted me to do. My at-home Bible study on fear had ended, and I found myself saying yes to leading a ladies' life group at my church. It was a DVD Bible study, and so the pressure was off to have to come up with a lesson every week. I would simply be "leading" the group in the study. It was intimidating to me, though, because it was not in my home anymore but in the church. And it was no longer my group of close friends, but it would be whoever happened to sign up for the group. Again, I had mixed feelings of exhilaration and fear. But I was stepping into a new adventure with God, and there was no feeling like it!

I began to think about the things that I had pondered months ago. Is there a bigger picture here? Could my life be used to glorify my God? Could the pain and fear of the last nine months be used to glorify God? What was it all about?

God?

Me?

Others?

I was excited as I saw the names being signed up on my life group list. Some of them I knew, and some of them I didn't know. Some that signed up were dear friends that had attended my very first summer Bible study!

And just like with my summer Bible study, my excitement gave way to panic and fear when that first night of the study finally came. I remember being in the room at church and hearing all the voices talking, and everyone was happy and excited, so they were quite loud. I remember thinking, *What am I doing here? Why did I think this was a good idea? I am not worthy enough to be leading these women anywhere or through anything!* So once again (because I need to learn some lessons more than once), God showed me that I was focusing on what I was feeling rather than focusing on who He is! And not only was I forgetting who God is, but also forgetting that this was something that He wanted me to do. So, it didn't matter what my limitations were because, in my weaknesses, God was going to shine the brightest. And He did!

It was no accident that the DVD study that I was leading was on the subject of heaven. As we went through the study, it encouraged me once again about where my late husband Rich was and what he was experiencing. It was also encouraging to the ladies in the group that had suffered devastating losses in each of their own lives. Most of all, God was glorified, and we were thankful and in awe of everything that He has planned for us once we leave this earth.

The life group was successful, and many new friendships were forged. God was answering the questions that I had about my life. Was there a bigger picture here? There definitely was. What was it all about? God? Yes, it was all about God and all that He has for us. Was it about others? Yes, it was beyond a doubt all about others and helping them and pointing them to Jesus. Could my life, widowhood, and pain be used to glorify God? It could be. I certainly did not ask for pain or hardship, but what I had been through gave me such a tender heart for the hurting. It was a degree of empathy that I could not have gotten any other way.

More importantly, I realized that this is what God had for me. This was what I was meant to do. God wants me to be a teacher. God wants me to teach women and encourage them. God wants me to help women, especially the hurting ones. And I have learned that everyone has hurts. Some people's hurts are obvious, and others' hurts are private and hidden. But pain is pain, and I am here to walk with people through their pain and help them see the comfort and peace they can find in God. God is the ultimate healer. He can heal hurts and restore us beyond anything that we can ever imagine. And because I have lived that, I can help show it to others.

My relationship with God developed in another way as

well. Throughout the fall, the ever-wise Pastor Sal (the same man who taught me the powerful prayer of "God, I don't want this, and I don't like this, but I trust You") started mentioning a short and yet profound prayer in his sermons. The prayer was, "Lord, break me and make me." From the first time I heard it, it caught my attention, and I couldn't get it out of my mind. It probably doesn't seem to make sense to you, does it? Let me explain.

The first phrase, "break me," means that I would be asking God to break down my will by any means possible. Why would I do that? Well, as my relationship with God had been progressing all summer, I was beginning to see more clearly. I was feeling the Holy Spirit speaking to me on a daily basis. I was discovering my true self for the first time, the person that God had created me to be. I was also discovering God more and just beginning to understand how great His love was for me and for all of mankind. After a while, things seemed to level out a bit. But I wanted more. I wanted to know God even more. I realized that the only thing standing in between me and a closer relationship with God was me, or more specifically, my stubborn will. My will that wanted to do things my way. My will that still enjoyed doing things that I knew displeased God. Even though I had been believing and trusting God and enjoying the deep peace and joy that came with it, there were still times when there were things that God required of me that I refused to do. I am, after all, only human.

Psalm 51:7–8 says, "Purify me from my sins, and I will

be clean …, give me back my joy again; you have broken me—now let me rejoice." I was fascinated by the last part of that verse, "You have broken me—now let me rejoice." The words "break me" were not something that my pastor had come up with by himself; they were actually in the Word of God to us! Also, it suggested that after the "breaking," there was rejoicing. I was convinced that after my breaking process, I would actually be happier and be a better person.

Further down in verse 10, it says, "Create in me a clean heart, O God. Renew a loyal spirit within me." I wanted to be renewed. I wanted my heart to be renovated. And writing this even now, one year later, I can look back and see where there were other times that I needed to be renewed. It is a continual process. God is always available to renew and refresh us! We only need to ask. This is what keeps us from getting stuck in a rut. It helps us from taking this wonderful life that God has given us for granted! It recharges our joy and gives us a fresh supply of peace. This renewing process from God also comes with some work to do as well. In order to be renewed, there are changes to make, and sometimes the changes aren't easy.

I wanted God to break me, clean me out, and renew and refresh me. I wanted Him to build me back to an even better person than I was before. And so, I began to ask Him to do just that. But what part of me needed to be broken? What part of me needed to be changed? To be honest, I couldn't think of anything that needed to be changed. In my arrogance, I had thought that I was pretty darn good right where I was at! But God had brought another Bible verse to my attention.

Psalm 139:23–24a says, "Search me, O God, and know my heart; test me and know my anxious thoughts. Point out anything in me that offends you." In reading this, I realized that this is the first part of the "breaking" process. I began to pray, "God, point out anything in me that offends You." Wow! Did that ever open my eyes! There were things in me that offended God, and right away, He showed me what one of them was. Notice that He did not show me everything in me that offended Him all at once! It would be so overwhelming! God is patient and kind, and He works on us gently, a little bit at a time. We will never be at the point where we are perfect this side of heaven. But every day we should be a little bit better than what we were the day before.

God showed me areas in my heart where I harbored resentment against certain people. Some of the feelings were so well-hidden that I was not even aware of them. It is amazing how we can lie to ourselves sometimes. I confessed those resentments to God and asked Him to help me forgive those people if they had hurt me in some way. Some of them had not hurt me. To be honest, I just did not like them. And that was wrong. Sometimes there are people who just "rub us the wrong way," so to speak. And we don't necessarily want to wish them harm, but we don't necessarily want to see them very happy either. We may even say to ourselves or to others, "I just don't care for them." As if that were okay. I would encourage you to think about something—that this is not the way that God wants us to live. God has told us in His Word that Jesus is our example and that we should strive to be like Him (1 Peter 2:21). If you believe that Jesus Christ is the Son of God and that He came to Earth to die as a sacrifice for our sins and to save us, could you imagine if Jesus had the attitude of having some people He "just didn't like"? What if He died for some, but not all? What if there were certain types of people that just rubbed Jesus the wrong way, and so He did not extend His salvation and forgiveness to them? What if you were one of those people that rubbed Jesus the wrong way, and so you were not eligible for His grace and forgiveness? As you are reading this, you might be thinking, *That's utterly ridiculous; Jesus loves everyone.* And that is so true! He does! And we, as believers, are called to love in the same way that Jesus does, with no exceptions!

I do not mean to make this sound like this is an easy thing to do, as the breaking process is hard. It is not easy when God reveals to you things that you need to change. My first reaction was to simply ignore what God was saying to me. This made me miserable. My second reaction was that it would be impossible for me to show that much love to people I didn't like. But I knew that, in my weak areas, God would give me strength. And finally, I defended my wrong feelings to God by saying, "But God, You know how impossible they are! You know how hard they are to love!" Can you believe I said that to God? Isn't that like I was saying to God that He had made a mistake when He created them because they weren't to my liking?

There was a whole process of me coming to the end of myself and my excuses, humbling myself before God, and admitting that I was wrong. I asked God to help me to see them the way Jesus sees them, and I asked God to give me the grace to love them. And He did. And He made sure to help me accomplish this by putting me in every possible situation with each and every one of them. You've got to love God's sense of humor!

I am now writing this a year later, and I can tell you that this was a lesson I had to learn again and again. I guess I am a slow learner in some areas! But I am thankful to God for His patience and lovingkindness to me.

The second part of my prayer after "break me" was for God to "make me." This is a short way of asking God that after He broke me down (and showed me the error of my ways), would He please now build me back and make me into a better person than I was before. I wanted my end result to be that I would be a little bit more like Jesus. Ezekiel 36:26 says, "I will give you a new heart, and I will put a new spirit in you. I will take out your stony, stubborn heart and give you a tender, responsive heart." God took away my stubborn heart and gave me a tender heart. And like I said before, this is a continual process and a lesson that I had to learn repeatedly. But each time got easier, and I learned in time to be less judgmental and to look at people sincerely through the eyes of Jesus.

So, what was the end result of this? Remember when I said before that even though I had a deep relationship with

God, I still wanted more and wanted to know Him more? What happened to me next can be summed up perfectly in Colossians 1:10, "Then the way you live will always honor and please the Lord, and your lives will produce every kind of good fruit. All the while, you will grow as you learn to know God better and better." I grew so much through this process, and I got to know God even better! And there is nothing like getting to know your creator and the lover of your soul even better than you did before! God already knows us and loves us completely, but He wants us to get to know Him better and to love Him more. And there is no feeling in the world like it!

If you have a relationship with Jesus, I would love to ask you—have you ever said a prayer like this? Would you even consider it? It would be the hardest and yet the best thing you could ever do. God is always in the process of molding and refining us, and it is up to us how far we allow Him to do this. Do we trust Him and allow Him to lead us through the difficult process of being changed and refined? Do we fight Him at every turn? Or do we flat out refuse to let Him change us at all? This is one of the important things that make the difference between a believer and a Jesus follower.

If you are reading this and you're not sure if you have a relationship with Jesus or if you even really believe all of this, then I am pleased that you even made it this far into the book! I hope you continue with me to the conclusion of my journey and what happened after that. I know that reading this book may not be what brings you directly to

Jesus, but it is my desire and prayer that this may be one step in your journey of many to eventually meeting Jesus! It is my sincerest hope that if you are reading this book and we don't know each other, I will be able to meet you face to face in heaven one day!

And so, as all of these exciting things were happening in my relationship with God, exciting things were happening in my relationship with Bob as well. At this point, we were hopelessly in love. The more we got to know each other, the more we realized how alike we were and how well suited we were to each other. God sure knew what He was doing when He brought us together! We were alike in so many ways; the way we viewed the world, the weird things we both took delight in, our shared love of movies, music, and especially books, our similar childhood experiences, our distrust of people based on the toxic people we had had in our lives, the negative way we viewed ourselves, our on-again/off-again relationship with Jesus, and our mutual experiences of living completely for ourselves and running away from God and where that got us in life.

I was at the part of my life where I was transforming from a "believer" to a "Jesus follower," and I was in love with a man who was in the middle of that transformation himself. This put our relationship on a level that I had never experienced in any other relationship before. The euphoria of being in love was made even more intense by a spiritual connection. It was absolutely overwhelming.

When I married Rich, I was not sure of his spiritual status, and it was not something that we had discussed in depth much. Throughout our marriage, I had begun a journey to God as the Holy Spirit worked on me and brought me closer to Him. As I began to realize that being a believer was not enough and that I needed to follow Jesus more in every aspect of my life, Rich and I began to experience a spiritual disconnect in our relationship as he simply did not understand what I was thinking and experiencing. Sometimes we had a downright difficult time as we were not on the same page as to who God was to both of us and where He should be in our lives.

After we had begun to attend Waymart Church, Rich opened up his heart to God and trusted in Jesus as his Savior. He started a relationship with His creator, and there was a change in him. One year later, he died unexpectedly and met God face to face. Knowing where he was and who he was with gave me peace beyond measure. It meant more to me than anything. It gives me peace even to this day.

Dear believer and skeptic alike, death is the most awful and dreadful thing. We fear it. We dread losing loved ones to it. We do everything we can to stay healthy and safe and live here on Earth as long as we are able. But sooner or later, we all die. Death is the ultimate separator. It separates us from our loved ones in a way that cannot be compared to anything else here on Earth, such as being apart by distance or a broken relationship. And once it is done, there is no way it can be undone. With every day that goes by, our chances increase of losing someone very close to us. And so, I ask you, how do you view death? Do you think about it much? Or do you prefer to ignore it and just wait to deal with it when it actually happens?

The Bible teaches us that if we are believers, we do mourn when we lose loved ones. We experience just as much pain and grief as anyone else. But we do it in a different way. First Thessalonians 4:13 (AMP) says, "We do not want you to be uninformed, believers, about those who are asleep [in death], so that you will not grieve [for them] as the others do who have no hope [beyond this present life]." In other words, we do grieve, but we grieve with hope. That hope is the belief that we will be reunited with our loved ones after death. Like I said before, death is the ultimate separator, but for believers, it is a temporary separation. For unbelievers, death is a permanent separation.

I can tell you from my experience that it was a subject that I did not spend too much time thinking about until I had no other choice. And it was knowing where Rich's soul was when he died and the fact that I would one day see him again that kept me from being completely destroyed by his death and living the rest of my life angry, sad, and bitter.

I said all that to say this; as I began my transformation from believer to Jesus follower, as I began to know God even more and in a more intimate way, I realized something I had never thought of before. If I were to ever have another relationship again, it would have to be in a relationship with someone who was on the same page as I was in that respect (2 Corinthians 6:14–15). That is exactly what God brought to me in Bob. And our relationship was one that exceeded any expectations that I had ever had about what a relationship should be.

Although Bob and I were not what you'd call young, we felt like teenagers. We had so much fun together, we laughed so much together, and we found so much joy in doing the simplest things as long as we were together. We talked for hour upon hour, read our Bibles together, and prayed together. Not only were we excited for what the future held for us, but we were excited for what God had in store for us as a couple. We encouraged each other spiritually and helped each other grow.

One of our favorite things to do was to watch a full moon together. And as it so happened that first October that we were together, there was a full moon at the end of the month that was very special. It was on Halloween night, October 31st, which hadn't happened since 1944. It was also a Hunter's Moon and a Blue Moon. We were very excited about seeing this and planned the perfect place to view it, a beautiful park where we loved to go and hike. Little did I know that it would be under this very breathtakingly beautiful and unique moon that Bob would get down on one knee and ask me to marry him! I was so overwhelmed I could barely tell him yes. So many emotions had washed over me at that moment; overwhelming love for this man, thankfulness to God for bringing him into my life and for all that God had done for me this entire year, the miraculous wonder that I could even feel so much joy after the tragic way my year had begun, and shock that I could fall so deeply in love after such a short period of time.

I also need to note that in the spirit of *Star Wars* that had permeated our relationship from the start, Bob had given me that night a *Star Wars* ring to temporarily seal our engagement! I loved it so much, however, that I have worn it every day since!

Back in April, I had read Ephesians 3:20 (AMP), which says,

> *Now to Him who is able to [carry out His purpose and] do superabundantly more than all that we dare ask or think [infinitely beyond our greatest prayers, hopes, or dreams], according to His power that is at work within us.*

I had decided then, in the middle of the darkest time in my life, to take God at His word and believe that He was everything He claimed to be. I had decided that if I trusted in Him, He could do more than I could ever pray for, hope for, or dream for. At that time, I could not even begin to imagine how that could even be possible, but still, I decided to believe it. Hope is a choice, not a feeling. And I chose hope. Now here I was, six months later, experiencing a life that I could not even have dreamed of. A life full of purpose, peace, and new love. How could this even be possible? That is the power of God. That is the greatness of the one who created the universe yet knows every minute detail of your life, the power of the one who lives outside of time yet holds you in every moment of your grieving. We cannot even begin to fathom what God can do for us if we give ourselves fully to Him and choose to trust Him.

CHAPTER 10: NOVEMBER

I went into November as a widow of ten months and now a newly engaged woman. It was crazy, and yet I felt as though everything was exactly as it should be. There was a dual set of emotions banging around inside of me; the sadness of facing the first Thanksgiving and Christmas without my first husband and the joy and excitement of going through the first Thanksgiving and Christmas with my new *fiancé*.

There were those close to me that questioned my judgment (which I completely understood) and those that walked with me through my journey of grief and healing that completely understood where I was coming from, and so they were very happy for me. I had already gone through my period of questioning myself and my judgment. I had prayed and prayed to God about my feelings for Bob and about if this was the right thing to do, and His answer was always yes. I do not say these words to you flippantly. I understand that what was happening to me was out of the ordinary and that the timeline in which it was happening was unconventional. I do not want you to get the impression that I was rushing into something and using "But God told me to do it" as an excuse. I had been married before and knew it was a decision that was not to be taken lightly!

They say hindsight is 20/20, and that is so right! Looking back now, I can see that the way that everything happened was exactly as God had planned it. But more of that in the last chapter of the book! Suffice it to say, I fully believed at that time that what God had for me was a life with Bob, and neither I (nor he) had any reservations about getting married.

I had something happen to me in November that further solidified in my mind that Bob was the right man for me and that he was brought to me by God. Proverbs 27:17 (AMP) says, "As iron sharpens iron, So one man sharpens [and influences] another [through discussion]." As I continued my journey from believer to Jesus follower and discovered what God's will was for my life, God was using Bob to help mold me. Bob was sharpening and influencing me in a godly way, and I was doing the same to him.

In November, I was invited to speak at a ladies' dinner at my church. I accepted this challenge excitedly, knowing that God was going to be with me every step of the way, from the studying and the message being prepared to standing before everyone and speaking it out. God had led me to speak to the ladies about the crazy events of 2020 and how He had chosen all of us for this time specifically to be a light for Him. This was not a study group of eight to ten ladies; this was going to be about sixty ladies, the biggest group I had spoken in front of yet! As I was driving to the church that evening, I had allowed my fear and anxiety to get the best of me. I thought that the group was too large and that this was beyond what I was capable of doing. I thought that the ladies all took time out of their evenings to come and have a delicious dinner, great fellowship, and an encouraging message and that I was *not* the one to be able to deliver what they had come to hear. I started crying and praying as I was driving, and then I thought, *I need to call Bob.* I pulled over on the side of the road and called him. I poured out my heart to him. He was so strong, so reassuring! He told me in his deep and calm voice that he believed in me and that he knew that I could do it. He also told me that he knew that God was with me and that I could do anything through Him. He said that he had peace in his heart, knowing that I was exactly where God wanted me to be and doing exactly what God wanted me to do. He asked me what time during the evening would I be speaking, and he promised me that, at that time, he was going to stop what he was doing and pray for me. He said exactly what I needed to hear. And although I walked into church that night very nervous, knowing Bob was at his house praying for me, knowing that he was in my corner, that he had my back, gave me the confidence I needed. I still remember sitting there as I was being introduced, feeling a huge wave of peace pass over me and my anxiety wash away. I walked up to that podium with a huge smile on my face, for there is no greater joy like the joy of being directly in the center of God's will for your life and doing exactly what He has called you to do!

I knew that God was with me that night and that, in my weakest moments, His amazing power shone through, but I also knew that Bob and his prayers had a hand in it too. That was the first time that I realized that not only had God brought Bob to me to love me but also to be an integral part of my spiritual growth as well. Bob was going to be a part of my refining process, helping me to become what God wanted me to be.

God tells us that He uses our relationships with others to help refine us. And in turn, we can help refine others as well. Relationships are a gift from God. Who are your closest relationships with? What are those relationships like? The people we spend our time with influence us greatly, probably even more than we realize.

The Bible has so much to say about relationships! For example, Proverbs 18:24 (AMP) says, "The man of too many friends [chosen indiscriminately] will be broken in pieces and come to ruin, But there is a [true, loving] friend who [is reliable and] sticks closer than a brother." Proverbs 27:9 (AMP) says, "Oil and perfume make the heart glad; So does the sweetness of a friend's counsel that comes from the heart."

And as far as our responsibility in dealing with our relationships with others, God commands us to "encourage each other and build each other up" (1 Thessalonians 5:11).

Throughout my life, I've had relationships with people that both encouraged me and discouraged me. In my experience with both, I have been able to learn and grow. But I am so thankful that in my most difficult time of being a widow, God had me in the right place at the right time. I was completely surrounded by people that encouraged me, took care of me, and built me up. I really could not have gotten through that time without them. They encourage me and build me up even until this day. And I pray that I am doing the same for them as well.

And in time, God blessed me with another uplifting and encouraging relationship, one that was deep and personal and intimate, one that was going to change my life. And that was Bob. I had the excitement of new love, but not only that, I had the excitement of God doing amazing things in my life, and Bob was a part of those amazing things. When I fully put my trust in God and opened my heart up to whatever He had planned for me, it opened up a whole new world for me. It opened up my eyes and I saw as I had never seen before. I see what is important in life and what is not. I see people in a different way, I see love in a different way, and most importantly, I see God in a different way.

Dear reader, I would like to encourage you to think about your relationships. Think about those that are closest to you. Do they encourage you or discourage you? Do they influence you to try to be a better person, or do they have a negative effect on you? And in that same vein, ask yourself how do you influence those around you? Just as you have friendships that build you up and sharpen you as iron sharpens iron, you may be the person building someone else up and sharpening them. Maybe you don't even realize how much they need you right now. Look around you. Don't take any acquaintance for granted. God created us for relationships! And a relationship with Him is the most important and most fulfilling of all!

And speaking of iron sharpening iron, I need to share with you an incident that happened to me with one of my friends, a very close friend that I had known for a very long time. Proverbs 27:5–6 says, "An open rebuke is better than hidden love! Wounds from a sincere friend are better than many kisses from an enemy." In other words, a friend who is a true friend will tell you what you need to hear even though it may not always be what you want to hear. A friend may rebuke you, which can wound you, but in the long run, it is for your own good. The Bible says that this is better than a so-called "friend" who only flatters and tells you what you want to hear and really does not care about your welfare. God calls that "kisses from the enemy," and He says that it is better to have "wounds from a sincere friend" than "kisses from an enemy."

Around this time, I had received a "wound from a sincere friend," and I must admit that in the beginning, I did not take it very well at all. I even considered severing all ties with that person! They had sent me a private message questioning my happiness with my new relationship, considering that I had only lost my first husband eleven months ago. They were totally confused at the way I was acting and were even angry to a certain extent with me. My first reactions were surprise and hurt. I was not naive; I knew that there were people questioning my judgment and feelings in all of this, but to actually see it in front of me made it real, and it stung. My second reaction was anger. I immediately started planning in my mind what kind of scathing message I would send back to that person, reminding them that they had no idea what I was going through and not to judge me until they had walked a mile in my shoes. I had thought of several snarky comebacks that I could send to them that would attack them and hurt them. Another thing I had thought of was to simply cut them off, block them from my social media, and ignore the fact that they had ever even existed. So much for me being a Jesus follower, right?

I had decided to wait a couple of days and think about things before I got back to them. That was the best thing I ever did because it gave me time to think about my friend and try to see things from their point of view. Looking at it from their point of view also made me rethink what I was feeling, what I was going through, and again pray about everything that was going on. I also thought about our many years of friendship and whether or not this message was worth enough to make me end it. The message itself was not mean, and it ended with the person telling me how much they loved me and were concerned for me. I thought about Proverbs 17:14 and 19, which says, "Starting a quarrel is like opening a floodgate, so stop before a dispute breaks out. …Anyone who loves to quarrel loves sin." I doubted that my friend was trying to be mean to me and was genuinely concerned, but even if they were trying to pick a fight—I knew that God would want me to answer them with kindness because "Kind words are like honey—sweet to the soul and healthy for the body" (Proverbs 16:24) and "A gentle answer deflects anger, but harsh words make tempers flare" (Proverbs 15:1).

I also thought that if I had other friends out there that felt this way, it was interesting that only this one particular friend had enough courage and was secure enough in our friendship to confront me about it. It had to be uncomfortable for them to do it.

I messaged my friend back and tried my best to explain exactly what I was thinking and feeling. I was as honest and transparent as I could possibly be. I also thanked them for being so honest with me. They were very happy with my response because my explanation helped them to understand more of what was going on. They understood me better now, and they were genuinely happy for me.

As we walk through life, we all have to remember that none of us know completely what anyone else is thinking or what their internal struggles may be. Like the saying, "Never judge a book by its cover," we should never judge others just by looking at their outer demeanor and not consider what may be going on on their inside. We may look at someone who, on the outside, seems to have it all together, and on the inside, they may be completely falling apart. Their souls may be crying out for help, but we don't sense it, and we are too focused on judging them based on what we are seeing and hearing from them. And although I don't condone calling out just any acquaintance on what we may perceive is unusual behavior from them, I do hope that everyone reading this has some close friends that they can talk to honestly and openly. Life can be very hard sometimes, and we need to be watching out for each other! And if you feel as though you don't have any friends that are that close, please know that Jesus is there for you. He is the closest friend you could ever have. He knows you more than anyone else ever has, and He loves you more than anyone else ever has or ever will. First John 3:16 says, "We know what real love is because Jesus gave up his life for us." There is nothing on the face of this planet that can take that love away from you—

> *(Not) death nor life, angels nor demons, ... not even the powers of hell. ...No power in the sky above or in the earth below ..., nothing in all creation will ever be able to separate us from the love of God that is revealed in Christ Jesus.*
>
> **Romans 8:38–39**

November was also the month I celebrated my birthday. I was fifty years old and spent most of that fiftieth year being a widow. It was not something that I was ashamed of. Widows and widowers come in all shapes, sizes, and ages. Widowhood is not for the faint of heart. It takes a huge amount of strength and courage to navigate the dark waters of widowhood. And God was with me every step of the way. I had assumed that I would be a widow for the rest of my life. And I was completely okay with it. That was the path that God had chosen for me. I knew that the rest of my life was going to be full of joy and peace no matter what happened next because God was in control and had a good plan for my life. Never in a million years could I have predicted that God was going to bring someone into my life, and so quickly too. Yet that is exactly what happened, and I was surprised, thrilled, and amazed.

Now that I was turning fifty-one, I felt as though I was turning the page to the end of a chapter and starting a new one in my life. That new chapter included planning a life together with Bob. Bob had contacted Pastor Sal and told him about our engagement news and asked him if he would counsel and marry us. Pastor Sal and his wife, Dena, had walked with me through my difficult journey right from day one. They also had known Bob for a very long time. They were very happy to hear we were dating. But dating someone and marrying them are two different things.

Pastor Sal was happy to meet with us but skeptical and cautious as well. Our unconventional story and speedy timeline did not concern him as much as whether or not it was God's will for the both of us. Bob and I were both very happy that he was so concerned about this, as it had been our concern all throughout our dating as well. Our first meeting was a long list of blunt questions that I was not expecting. Pastor Sal had married enough couples and also counseled enough couples in trouble that he knew exactly what red flags to look for. He did not beat around the bush! He was to the point and gave us a lot to think about. Some of our counseling sessions were rough, and I felt like he was being unfair. Proverbs 25:12 says, "To one who listens, valid criticism is like a gold earring or other gold jewelry." In time I realized that Pastor's "valid criticism" was very valuable, that it was things that absolutely needed to be said at the time, and that it was all coming from a place of love. Pastor Sal loved us, wanted to see us living under God's blessing, and did not want to see us making a mistake.

One serious concern of Pastor Sal's was how my children were feeling about all of this, and he asked to have one counseling session with them alone, followed by another session with all four of us. You may be wondering where my children were in all of this as well. Out of respect for them and their feelings, I had decided from the beginning of writing about my journey not to include their stories in my book. This is my story, my thoughts, my feelings, and I would never even begin to try to describe what I thought either of them was going through. I talked with them, asked them questions, and had a front-row seat to the suffering they went through, but the complexities of their innermost thoughts and feelings are their own private journeys, their story to tell (if they ever choose to share), and not mine.

One thing that I can say for sure is that, right from the beginning of all of this, their strength of spirit, their steadfast faith, and how they have conducted themselves throughout the whole ordeal and beyond have completely blown me away. I do not know and cannot even imagine how kids their age are supposed to act when their dad dies and so unexpectedly at that. I was, and still am, in awe of them. My relationship with Bob had progressed so quickly that I feel as though they were always trying to catch up to everything, and a lot of the time, they probably felt lost or left behind. But they handled our relationship and our decision to get married with grace and dignity. They miss their dad so much; there are no words to describe it. I also know that they love their mom and want her to be happy.

Although Bob and I were already planning a life together and believing that God had His blessing upon us, we were still waiting for Pastor Sal's seal of approval. Without his blessing, we would have to stop and rethink everything that we were doing. Pastor Sal knew us both well. Both Bob and I had grown spiritually by leaps and bounds through his teaching at Waymart Church. His opinion mattered. If Pastor Sal did not have peace about us getting married, then we would have to question why we were having peace. We would wonder if we were getting carried away by our emotions and not thinking rationally. So, you can imagine how thrilled we were when Pastor informed us that he would be happy to marry us and that he had no reservations whatsoever. And so, we began to think about getting married the following year.

And the next thing I knew, it was Thanksgiving. I do agree that time seems to drag when you are going through painful times, and time flies when you are having fun, but overall, time itself passes by very quickly. Life goes by so fast! James 4:14 says, "Your life is like the morning fog—it's here a little while, then it's gone." Psalm 144:4 says, "(You) are like a breath of air; (your) days are like a passing shadow."

Thanksgiving was certainly different for me that year. How could I possibly be thankful for the way my year had begun, and yet, there were still so very many things to be thankful for. First Samuel 12:24 says, "Be sure to fear the Lord and faithfully serve him. Think of all the wonderful things he has done for you." And so, I thought of everything that God had done for me all year. First of all, even though God had chosen to take Rich home, I was so thankful that Rich knew Jesus, and I knew where he was and that I would see him again. And then the list went on. There were so many things to be thankful for it was overwhelming. God had been with me all year and had never left me. God had taken care of my children and me in every way you could possibly imagine. God had called me closer to Him than I had ever been in my life, and I experienced peace in my soul that I had never felt before. God had given me a new calling of teaching ladies and ministering to them and all the joy that goes along with that. God had given my son and daughter the strength and courage to go on and to shine their lights for Him. And finally, God had given me Bob, a man to love me and take care of me and for me to love back. God had given me a new kind of love, one that was rooted in both of us seeking Him first, looking out for each other second, and taking care of ourselves last. It was a type of relationship that I had not ever experienced before.

First Thessalonians 5:18 says, "Be thankful in all circumstances, for this is God's will for you who belong to Christ Jesus." And I did learn how to be thankful to God in *all* circumstances, and not just when my circumstances were good and going according to the way that I thought they should be. Thankfulness is not a warm feeling that you get when everything around you is going well; thankfulness is a decision you make. In just about every circumstance, no matter what is going on, you can still find something (many things) to be thankful for. The choice is yours whether or not you want to look for those things.

If you believe in Jesus Christ as your Savior, if you have a genuine relationship with Him, then let me encourage you to always make that the number one thing on your list to be thankful for. No matter what kind of difficult situation you are going through, it means everything to know that you never walk alone, that there is one who walks with you, who created you, who loves you more than you'll ever know, and who has a good plan for your life, no matter how things may look in the moment.

Psalm 86:12–13 says, "With all my heart I will praise you, O Lord my God. I will give glory to your name forever, for your love for me is very great. You have rescued me from the depths of death." There is also a great amount of peace and thankfulness we can have in knowing that our eternity has been set, our salvation is sure, and that when the time comes for us to leave this earth, we know where we're going and that we will be with Jesus. We will also be reunited with loved ones that we love and miss so much. This is the bottom line. Even if you could not find one single thing in your current circumstances to be thankful for, you have this.

Beyond that, there are still so many things to be thankful for! Just the fact that you wake up every morning is something to be thankful for because as long as you are alive and breathing, God still has great plans for you!

If you are not sure how much of this to believe, whether it is all true or not, I would like to encourage you to think about the things you are thankful for. Look at things from a positive point of view. Consider this, God's love is as "vast as the heavens" (Psalm 36:5), and that love is for *you*. Psalm 36 also goes on to say that "You care for people and animals alike, O Lord. How precious is your unfailing love, O God! All humanity finds shelter in the shadow of your wings" (verses 6–7). If you are going through a difficult time, if you are fearful, sad, or anxious, if you need peace, find shelter in God. Look to Him for help. Tell Him all about your problems, about how you are feeling. God says that *all* humanity will find shelter in the shadow of His wings, and this includes you.

CHAPTER 11: DECEMBER

With December came the excitement of the holiday season. If you are mourning the loss of a loved one, Christmas seems to be the most difficult time to get through. There almost seems to be something so wrong about everyone being so happy and celebratory while your loved one is not celebrating because they are gone. It is hard watching everyone be happy and excited, and it seems like they don't notice your emptiness and grief. I completely understand. Both my kids and I were facing our first Christmas without Rich. Since Rich enjoyed Christmas so much, part of me felt bad that he wasn't here to experience it, and yet the other part of me knew that he was having his best Christmas yet, as it was being spent with the one for whom we celebrate Christmas, the Lord Jesus Christ Himself!

I would like to have all of my readers stop for a moment and consider this often-heard saying, "Life is for the living." We have heard it, read it, and used it ourselves. It is so often repeated that I'm not sure we truly grasp the meaning of it. I came to the realization in December that life really and truly is here on Earth for the living. Once a loved one is gone, there is no way we can have them living here on Earth with us again. They have gone from living on Earth to a whole new life of eternity. An eternity that our finite human hearts cannot even begin to imagine. An eternity that we will eventually be joining them in. Life is so short, but what happens after that is *forever*. I'm not even sure we can truly grasp the idea of forever.

There are so many ways that I hope and pray this book can help encourage others, but the most important thing I want for each reader is for them to consider life after death and where they will be spending eternity. If you get nothing else out of this book, just please know that everyone has to spend forever somewhere (Pastor Sal's quote, not mine). It is my hope and prayer that this book will encourage those that have a relationship with Jesus to be strengthened in their faith and to know that whatever happens to them in this life, they will be able to handle it with grace and courage that they never knew possible through the strength that comes from God.

For those that aren't sure how much of this they believe, who aren't sure if they have a relationship with Jesus, who aren't sure where they will be spending eternity, it is my hope and prayer that my experience has piqued your interest enough to search for God and look for answers. Discovering (and being found by) God is the most fulfilling journey you will ever make. If you have any questions or want to talk to me more about this, feel free to e-mail me at larissitude@gmail.com.

And since life is for the living, since it is a gift from God, I chose to celebrate Christmas to the best of my ability. We (our new family comprised of myself, Bob, Dale, and Cheyenne) put up a tree (which included Bob's ornaments as well as ours), decorated, and bought gifts. We rearranged our schedules, did things a little differently, and started new traditions. It was different from what all four of us had ever known, and it turned out to be a nice Christmas.

Christmas Eve at the Waymart Church was beautiful and joyous. Bob was the bass player on our church's worship team, and I was so proud of him and his music. The whole team did a wonderful job, and I was so moved. It made me realize just how awesome, how incredible the gift of Jesus Christ to the world really is. It means everything to me; it was strength for this past year, it is hope for my tomorrow, and the anticipation of seeing Rich and all my loved ones that had passed away in heaven again someday. Knowing and truly understanding this allowed me to have a very special and joyful Christmas despite the fact that I was actually anticipating it to be painful and difficult. Again, this was something that many people who knew me could not understand, and I totally get that because it was something I could not even explain myself. But that is the awesomeness of God and the amazing things that He can do in our lives. The Bible says that God can give us peace that "passes human understanding," and that is exactly what it is, peace in the midst of difficult circumstances that we cannot understand or explain, and yet it *is* there, and it *is* real. I have experienced it firsthand myself.

Early Christmas morning, when it was just myself, my son, and my daughter, I gave them each a teddy bear made from their dad's flannel shirts. We had a time together of remembering and mourning first thing that morning, but then we moved on to the present time with the arrival of Bob. I was concerned at the beginning about how Christmas was going to go, but it ended up being a very warm and enjoyable Christmas, filled with surprises and laughter, one that I will never forget.

It was around this time that we also finished our pre-marital counseling with Pastor Sal. The next step was to decide when to get married. Since January 29th would be the one-year anniversary of Rich's death, it was almost impossible to come up with a wedding date. We went in circles trying to figure out what day would be "appropriate" and could come up with no answers. We finally decided that since the year 2020 was the year of sadness and life changes, we were going to make the year 2021 the year of happiness and hope and that the happiness and hope were going to start immediately. So we first picked January 1, 2021, as the day we would get married, but then settled on January 3, 2021, as it was a Sunday, and we could get married immediately after the church service. It would be a small and simple ceremony and open to anyone who wanted to share our day with us.

After Christmas Day, I had time to sit and think and reflect on the past year and what a year it had been. It was truly a year of incredible highs and gut-wrenching lows. It was hard to believe how quickly the year had passed. It was hard to believe I had survived it all. It was hard to believe my kids had survived it all. It was hard to believe I had fallen in love and was about to get married. It was hard to believe how much my relationship with God had evolved and how, for the first time in my life, I was really beginning to understand what a relationship with God truly meant and how wonderfully and crazily joyous it was to live every day fully aware of His presence in me, through me, and all around me.

It is so hard to sum up the year in words, but Psalm 71:20–22 pretty much describes it all,

> *You (God) have allowed me to suffer much hardship, but you will restore me to life again and lift me up from the depths of the earth. You will restore me to even greater honor and comfort me once again. Then I will praise you ...because you are faithful to your promises, O my God.*

God did indeed allow me to suffer much hardship. He lifted me up out of my grief and gave me life again. He comforted me and never left me. He not only gave me my life back again but on an even greater level than before. Please don't misunderstand me! I am not saying my life got better after Rich passed away! I am saying that I got better. And my relationship with God got better. And one of the results of a better relationship with God was really and truly understanding where Rich is right now and how wonderful it is for him. Remember how I said that true joy does not have to do with the circumstances around you but that it has to do with what is going on inside you? That is what I was experiencing.

You see, my long-time relationship with God was what I would have considered shallow and, therefore, non-fulfilling. I was not in it 100 percent. I believed with my head but not fully with my heart. I had head knowledge of who God was but had not experienced it in my soul. This was because I did not fully put my trust in Him. I was definitely a child of God but not living for God. I had trusted Jesus Christ as my Savior, but I was not a Jesus follower. I had lived every day the best way I knew how instead of trusting God and allowing Him to lead me every moment of every day into the kind of life I never could have imagined.

Because my relationship with God was shallow and was not deeply rooted in complete trust in Him, I did not have true joy in my soul. My joy was dependent on what was going on around me. Yes, I did have some very happy times during my life, but that was not enough to carry me through the unhappy times. And I had plenty of unhappy times due to the fact that I had always lived for myself instead of putting God and others first. My happiness depended on everything around me going the way that I wanted it to go.

But when I had decided to put God first, completely trust who He claimed to be, and embrace everything He had in life for me, that's when things changed. I really began to know God on a deeper level, and this filled me with joy that I had not experienced ever in my life. This was a true joy that could not be snuffed out by any kind of heartache or tragedy. In fact, it was this joy and peace that got me through the heartache and tragedy. This love and joy that filled me overflowed to those around me. I see people more clearly and love them more deeply. It is an entirely different existence than I had ever known.

That is what I mean when I say that God not only gave me my life back, but He gave me a life back on an even greater level than I had known before. I had finally learned that true joy has to do with what is inside you, not what is going on around you on the outside. Because of this, I was able to experience great happiness and joy in what should have been the most unhappy and difficult year of my entire life.

It took a tragedy to get my attention, and I pray, dear reader, that it will not be the same way for you. Remember back in my book when I told you that "God shows us He is in control by putting us in circumstances that we can't control"? That is what He did. And at that time, I had two choices; to decide to trust God and allow Him control of my life or to turn my back on God, let my circumstances make me angry and bitter, and try to control my life myself. I cannot even begin to tell you how happy I am that I decided to put my trust in God and believe that He is everything He claims to be. He certainly is that! He is that and so much more! He tells us in His Word that "no mind has imagined what God has prepared for those who love him" (1 Corinthians 2:9), and it is so true! You can't imagine what God has planned for you! No dream is too big! Not only will God do things in your life that you can't even begin to imagine, but we have a whole eternity waiting for us that we can't even begin to imagine either!

And so, I ask you, believer, who is God in your life, and how much do you trust Him? You may be only one decision away from living a kind of life that you only could have dreamed of. Please think back on the words that you have been reading throughout this book. Remember my journey that you have just gone through with me and know this; God is exactly who He claims to be in His Word and that He is 100 percent completely worthy of us putting our full trust in Him and putting Him first in our lives! Your life is a gift from God, and living that life in full abandon for Him is the best thing you can possibly do with that gift.

If you are a believer but going through a very painful time right now; if you've had the rug ripped out right from under you as I did; if you are in the middle of circumstances that are way out of your control or even your ability to cope, you may be asking yourself right now if God is worthy of your trust. Let me assure you, He is! Remember the prayer, "God, I don't want this, and I don't like this, but I trust You"? Start with that prayer. Choose to trust. I believe it will be the lifeline that you have been waiting for.

CHAPTER 12: JANUARY...
ONE YEAR LATER

And just like that...the year of loss and life change had ended, and I was determined that this new year would be the year of happiness and hope. Psalm 16:8 says, "I know the Lord is always with me. I will not be shaken, for he is right beside me." And that is exactly where He was. He was right beside me every step of the way during the past year. And as I stepped into the new year, I had complete confidence that He would continue to be with me, no matter what the future held.

The middle part of that verse says, "I will not be shaken," but I must admit, I did indeed get shaken! I got scared, and I got worried, and I felt unsure. The whole year was not me bravely marching through tragedy undaunted. There were times of crippling fear and uncertainty. There were times of curling up on my bed in the fetal position. There were times when I did not think I could go on for one more minute. But there were also times of great peace.

There were times when I was able to do things fearlessly that surprised even me. There were times of strength that was so supernatural it could only have come from God. Second Corinthians 4:8–9 says, "We are pressed on every side by troubles, but we are not crushed. We are perplexed, but not driven to despair. ...We get knocked down, but we are not destroyed." I was indeed pressed by trouble, but it never crushed me! (Although, at times, it felt like I was going to be crushed.) I was certainly perplexed and confused, but I did not despair! And life had certainly knocked me down, but I was not destroyed! And sitting here writing this today, I now know that I will *never* be destroyed! I am a child of God! And Romans 8:31b says, "If God is for us, who can ever be against us?"

I'm sure you have heard the saying that "God is my co-pilot." In my case, God is my pilot. And there are times when all I can do is buckle up, hold on tight, put my trust completely in Him, and enjoy the wild and exhilarating ride!

I stepped into the new year confident and stronger in my faith than I had ever been. I knew that whatever my future held, it was going to be okay because I knew who held me in the palm of His hand, and I was loved and protected.

I stepped into the new year abundantly blessed by God, surrounded by His love, and filled with joy.

I stepped into the new year in love with Bob, being loved by him, and excited about starting a life with him. Our wedding day, however, almost didn't happen as we got a blizzard that morning! Bob came to my house and picked up Dale, Cheyenne, and me, and it was a treacherous ride to the church. Most of the people that had planned on going were unable to make it because of the bad roads. It was a very small and intimate group for the wedding.

Sitting through the church service with Bob before our wedding was surreal, and I could not stop praising God and being thankful for all that He had done for me. I kept thinking about the Bible verse that says, "And we know [with great confidence] that God [who is deeply concerned about us] causes all things to work together [as a plan] for good for those who love God" (Romans 8:28, AMP). That was what I was experiencing. God works *all* things (the good and the bad) out as a plan for good for us. I don't know how He does it, but He does. It's supernatural. It's more than what we can understand. When we trust Him, we will see it and experience it. Trust is a choice; we decide to either trust God through tough circumstances where we can't see any way out or turn our back on Him.

When Rich first died, I kept thinking, *Why did God do this to me?* As if God calling Rich home was something that God did personally to me for some reason. I do not know why God chose that specific day and time to end Rich's life on Earth and take him home to heaven. Someday I will know.

Rich dying was not something good that happened to me. It is a loss I will always carry with me. But my life is good; in fact, it is great. God has caused good in my life through this tragedy. God will continue to cause good in my life no matter what circumstances arise if I continue to trust Him.

And so, less than one year after losing my first husband, I was marrying my second husband.

Our ceremony was short and sweet and full of love, love for each other, and love for God. We had asked Pastor Sal to read Ecclesiastes 4:12, "A person standing alone can be attacked and defeated, but two can stand back-to-back and conquer. Three are even better, for a triple-braided cord is not easily broken." This verse means so much to us as Bob and I feel we can stand back-to-back and conquer this crazy thing we call life, but more importantly, having God with us, we are a triple-braided cord that cannot be broken.

And now, you have come with me full circle on my journey. What are you thinking at this point? Are you happy for me? Are you skeptical? Are you picturing this moment like the ending of a movie? Bob and I walking off into the sunset hand in hand while "The End" rolls across the screen and the music swells? Do you think we lived "happily ever after"? Well, hang on to your hats because nothing is ever quite as it seems...

CHAPTER 13: HAPPILY EVER AFTER?

Psalm 34:19 says, "The righteous person faces many troubles, but the Lord comes to the rescue each time." Notice that this verse says "many" troubles, not one or two troubles, not one great catastrophe that is followed by smooth sailing if you make it through; it says *many* troubles. Also, notice that it says that the Lord comes to rescue *each* time. Not some of the time, not many times, not only when you're being good, but *each* time. Life is a series of trials, and like I said before, trusting in God does not mean that you will never have any trials, but it does mean that you will never go through those trials alone.

I walked into the new year with the confidence of knowing that God is always with me and that "I will not be shaken, for he is right beside me" (Psalm 16:8), but once again, I was shaken; I had something happen to me that shook me to my very core.

There is no need to go through all the drama of all the tests, scans, and biopsies that lead up to this moment, but on May 7th, four months and four days after Bob and I were married, I got a phone call saying that I had been diagnosed with breast cancer.

I had gotten this call while out in the middle of dinner in a restaurant with some friends from church. Among those friends were Pastor Sal and his wife Dena and some other friends that had been close to me throughout my journey last year. They were friends that cried with me when Rich died and were happy for me when Bob and I had found each other. One of the ladies was from my very first Bible study at my house last summer. Among the group were also three cancer survivors and one person currently battling cancer. These people were not just good friends, they were my family, and it was such a blessing to be able to be with them when I got my bad news. God certainly knows exactly how to take care of us through every moment of every second of our lives. When I shared my news with the group, I not only had friends to cry with, but four of them who actually knew exactly what I was going through as they had gone through the same thing themselves. God comforts us so that when we come in contact with others going through the same thing, we can comfort them as no one else can! We can comfort them with the same love and support that God gave to us in our time of need!

I must, however, tell you about mine and Bob's ride home. As you have been reading my book and going on my journey with me, you have seen the transformation that I have been through. You have seen my trust in God and my faith remain strong, and you have seen where that has taken me.

At this point, you might be impressed with me, and you might look at me as a "brave" or "courageous" woman, a strong "woman of faith," someone that you might even say, "I wish I could be like that." Well, I hate to burst your bubble, but guess what this "courageous woman of faith" did when she got in the car alone with her husband? Did I pray? Did I remain strong? Did I encourage myself and my husband to trust God to carry us through this? No. I did not. Instead, I threw a fit. A loud, sobbing, anger-filled fit.

So much for being a brave, courageous, strong woman of faith, huh?

I simply could not believe that God had allowed this to happen to me. It was like the same feeling I had when Rich died a year ago. I just could not get over the fact that God had allowed this. I could not imagine why God would have brought me through this past year just to let me die now from cancer. I could not imagine why God would let Bob and I find each other, just to let me die and leave Bob alone again. I could not imagine why God would take Dale and Cheyenne's dad away and now, a year later, take away their mom as well. Do you notice how I keep using the word "I"? I kept trying to figure this out; I kept trying to put this situation in a way that I could understand. As I had done in the past, I again focused on what my emotions were feeling instead of focusing on God and who He is.

And so, on that ride home from the restaurant, Bob

and I had an angry, tear-filled, ranting, and raving pity party. Our words to God were loud and filled with hurt and frustration. And where was God? He was right there with us. He held us. He listened to our words. He was there, and He never left us. Our words of anguish were not falling on deaf ears, not floating out unacknowledged into the atmosphere, but were being heard by the one who created both of us and loved us more than either one of us could ever imagine. And as both of us were crying and feeling abandoned, we both knew in the core of our beings that we belonged to God, that He loved us, that He was holding us in the palm of His hand, and that nothing was going to happen to us that wasn't in His perfect plan for both of our lives.

That moment in the car was what our initial gut reaction was to the situation.

I could have easily left this part out. I could have let you imagine that as a strong couple of faith, Bob and I took this all in stride and continued on in our faithful walk with God. But that is not what happened. From the start, I wanted my story to be genuine and honest, so I must share with you exactly what happened, my good moments and my not-so-good moments. I want to share my failures as well as my triumphs.

I share this because I want everyone reading this to know that we will all have our triumphs and failures. And that God will always love each one of us no matter how many times we falter in our faith, no matter how many times we make mistakes, or how many times we trip and fall down. He does not love us only when we are good. He does not withhold His love when we make mistakes. His love is 100 percent unconditional and eternal. We do nothing to earn His love, it is there, and it always has been, and there is nothing we can do that can take His love away. When we as humans are at our ugliest, God loves us just as much as when we are at our best. It is hard to even comprehend, but believing it and allowing it to permeate every ounce of our existence is the best thing we can ever do for ourselves.

Dear believer, I would encourage you to always remember that there is nothing you can do that will make God love you any more than He does right now. His love for you is complete. It's bigger than you could ever imagine! Live your life every day with that truth in your mind and in your heart.

For those who are unsure, I would encourage you today to go to God and tell Him that you want that kind of love, that you want His love, that you believe there is no greater love than the love that God has for you because He even sent His only Son Jesus to die for you. Believe it and receive it!

Like I had said before, that moment on the ride home was what our initial reaction was to the situation, but as time went on, both of us were able to process the situation and think clearly.

I thought a lot about the past year, what I had been through, and the fact that God had never abandoned me. I knew He was not abandoning me now. I knew He would *never* abandon me. I thought about the fear and the pain of last year and how Jesus had walked with me through it all. I thought about how I not only managed to survive my tragedy but that I had thrived in the midst of it. I knew that whatever happened next, Jesus would be right there with me just as He had always been. Little by little, I began to feel my fear disappear. I began to realize that nothing was going to happen to me physically that God did not already know about and that He was not going to allow. Once again, I had to remember that God was in control, and I was not. I had lived the previous year in perfect peace, knowing that God was in control. I wanted that peace again; I needed it. And so, once again, I chose to put my trust in God and not let my fear and anxiety overtake me.

I was scheduled for a full mastectomy and lymph node removal six weeks later. In the meantime, Bob and I had decided to do a Bible study that summer in our home on the book of 1 Peter, which talks about suffering and trials and how Jesus gives us supernatural peace in the midst of it, and how our trials ultimately draw us closer to Him. What a wonderful group we had for that study! It was exactly what I needed to help me prepare for what was coming. I've said this before, and I'll say it again; God cares for every minute detail of our life, and He always surrounds us with and supplies us with everything we need for each moment. What a blessing our small, intimate group was for me! I still remember the night they all put their hands on me and prayed for me. To this day, I can still feel that supernatural feeling of God's peace and presence that had washed over me as all of them held me and prayed. It was a powerful moment. It was a moment where I felt God so strongly that I got a tiny glimpse of what it must be like to be in His presence in heaven. And although I know that my brain cannot even fully comprehend what it must be like, my heart knows for sure that there will be nothing like it!

I can say for certain that I went into surgery that morning confidently and fearlessly. I had complete confidence in my surgeon. She is a skilled, competent, and strong woman and will always be my hero. I knew I was in good hands with her, and even more so, in the hands of God Himself. And even as I had woken up later to the sad news that the cancer was in my lymph nodes as well, both Bob and I knew for certain that God was in control, and we were not. And we chose to trust Him.

That overnight stay in the hospital was amazing for many reasons. First of all, I had not needed any painkillers that night, and even the nurses who took care of me were surprised about that. Secondly, I lay awake in bed most of the night in the presence of God. I mean, *really* in the presence of God. It was so strong that I felt as though I could almost see Him, feel His breath on me, feel His hand on me. It was surreal. I was so peaceful, so joyous, and so excited about it! It was so wonderful that I now know with most certainty that once I die and I am in His presence, it will be the most powerful and amazing thing that my existence has ever known.

As a believer, I know that God is always with me, but

there are times when I feel His presence more strongly than others. This is due to the fact that I am only human, that I get busy, I forget about Him, and I neglect my relationship with Him. But He is always there. And it seems to me that when I am at my weakest points, and I am most scared, I feel Him the strongest. Psalm 34:18 says, "The Lord is close to the brokenhearted," and that is so true! I have had people say to me, "I don't know how you got through all of that," but I know exactly how I got through it; it was God with me, in me, and all around me! This makes me want to follow Jesus even more, to pursue God even more, through prayer and through reading His Word and serving Him, so that I can feel this closeness with Him always. Not just in my weakest moments, but in every moment of my life!

Third, I had such a strong feeling of love and care for the staff that took care of me that night that it was overwhelming. Nurses are some of the most awesome people to walk in this world. They are special people. The nurses that took care of me that night have so many sick and dying to take care of that I am sure they have forgotten about me at this point. But I will never forget them or stop praying for them.

Two days later, I returned to the surgeon for a post-op check-up only to find out that my drainage tubes were blocked, and I had to have surgery again to open everything back up and drain all the blood out. My surgery was scheduled for that same day, late afternoon. There was nothing Bob or I could do except drive home and wait the day out. This was disappointing news for sure. It was not what we were expecting. I certainly did not want to go into surgery again. On the ride home, I once again felt the presence of God so strongly, but this time I was able to share it with Bob. He felt it too. We both agreed that it was surreal and a feeling completely out of this world. We felt such peace and were not upset that I had to go into surgery again. We knew I was in God's hands. God's presence was felt by both of us so strongly that it felt as if He was sitting in between Bob and me in the car!

We trusted that God had a reason for allowing this to happen, and we both believe that one of the reasons is because Bob (unknowingly) had an appointment (scheduled by God) with another man in the waiting room whose wife was also in surgery. Bob was able to have a conversation with this man, share his faith in God, and encourage him. If I did not need that second surgery, they never would have met. Bob will never forget his encounter with that man that day, and we will always remember him and pray for him and his wife.

Back in my chapter about November, I had told you about how Bob and I were planning on getting married. I told you that we both knew that it was very quick, and yet both Bob and I felt that everything was as God had planned it and that it was in His time. I know now without a doubt that God brought Bob to me at this time for a reason. He knew that I would need Bob for what was coming. I cannot imagine what my life would have been like that summer going through my cancer fight without

Bob by my side. He was there for me in so many ways, from just being there for me and holding me when I cried to changing my bandages, helping me bathe, praying for me, and being my spiritual counselor throughout it all.

Obviously, that is not the only reason that God brought Bob to me. It was His plan for us to meet, become friends, fall in love, and get married. It did, however, happen incredibly fast. When Bob and I really started to have feelings for each other, we knew we wanted to eventually get married and share a life together. There was no reason to be in a hurry to do this, and yet we felt such an urgency to get married quickly. We both shared these feelings with each other, and we couldn't explain why we both had the same feeling. It was not something we shared with anyone else because it didn't really seem to make sense. And yet the feeling was there, and it was undeniable. We now know why we felt the need to get married so quickly; we had to be together to face this disease head-on as a team. Being told that you have cancer is a feeling that is hard to imagine unless you have personally been through it. In a word, it is terrifying. It is a special kind of fear that gets a grip on you and does not let go. When I was told I had cancer, I was shocked, I was devastated, but most of all, I was so afraid. I am so thankful I had Bob to go through this with me. He was my rock. As it says in the book of Ecclesiastes, which was read at our wedding, two people together can stand back-to-back and fight, and that is just what we did. It goes on further to say that three are even better than two because a triple-braided cord is not easily broken, and it was not only Bob and I going through this, but God was with us as well. And we were not broken.

I would also like to add that besides the cancer battle, the rest of our first year of marriage had its ups and downs as well. Although we had not regretted for one moment when we got married, we did indeed get married quickly. We knew each other enough to know that we were meant to spend the rest of our lives together, but because we moved so quickly, there were still a lot of things we didn't know. There were areas where we misunderstood each other and clashed, and we had to learn as we went along. I do not regret any of those difficult moments at all, as they have only served to make us so much stronger. We have found that the most important thing in our relationship was that we each put God first in our lives, and we put each other ahead of ourselves. Like 1 Corinthians 13:7 says, "Love never gives up, never loses faith, is always hopeful, and endures through every circumstance."

Losing Rich taught me that I could trust God no matter how painful and difficult my circumstances might be, and having cancer taught me that I can trust God with my very life.

Psalm 34:19 says, "The righteous person faces many troubles, but the Lord comes to the rescue each time." Right now, after surgery and treatment, I am cancer-free. I do not know what my future holds, but I am not naive enough to think that life is going to be all good from here on in. In fact, the Bible tells me to expect trouble from time to time. But the Bible also reassures me that I will *never* walk through trouble alone.

If you are a believer, I want to remind you that being a Christian does not mean a trouble-free life. There are no exceptions to this. But I do want you to know that if you place your trust in God, there is no challenge you will not be able to overcome, no tragedy you will not be able to survive, there is nothing you will not be able to do when you have God with you! If you are going through a tough time right now, I encourage you not to ask why but to ask God, "What is next for me?" It could be your chance to do things that you never thought you were capable of doing; it could be your chance to shine for God, bring glory to His name, and point others to Him.

If you have come to the end of my book and want to make sure that you have a relationship with God, that you are part of His family, and that you will be spending eternity with Him once you leave this earth, I would encourage you to go to Him now. Do not wait another day. There are no certain words that you need to say, just go to Him and tell Him:

- That you believe that He loves you more than you ever could imagine.
- That you want to love Him in return and serve Him.
- That you believe that Jesus died for you and that He is the *only* way to have a relationship with God.
- Ask Jesus to be your Savior, believe in Him as such, and receive God's love.

Back in chapter 4 (May), I had talked about getting a feeling that maybe there was a bigger picture here, that there was more going on than what I was seeing in front of me. I had said that Rich dying was not a good thing, but that good could come from my painful circumstances. God really began to change my heart, and I began to feel such an overwhelming need to help people. I did not know how, but I felt such a need to reach people, to help people, to show them how much God loved them. Through teaching others in my Bible studies and through personal interaction, I have been able to do this. But this book is the biggest way yet for me to reach people.

Back in November, when Bob and I were doing pre-marital counseling with Pastor Sal, we were both giving him our individual stories and the story of how we came together. Pastor Sal looked at me and said, "Wow, you have quite a story; you should write a book." He then added, jokingly, "You should call it *How to Go from a Widow to a New Bride in under a Year*." As soon as he said it, I felt a jolt in my spirit, and I knew, I really *knew*, that this was what I was going to do. I knew what God wanted me to do. It didn't matter that I had never written a book, short story, or even a newspaper article. God wanted me to do it, and all He wanted from me was that I was willing to trust Him in this next challenge. I began writing right after Bob and I got married. I am so excited to write this book and share my story with you. Right from the start, I had always asked God to help me to reach as many people as possible with my story of His great love for me. I asked

God to help me reach as many people as possible to show them how much He loved them. And now it has finally happened!

My whole experience, including what may come in the future, can be summed up in this passage in the book of Psalms,

> *I waited patiently for the Lord to help me, and he turned to me and heard my cry. He lifted me out of the pit of despair, out of the mud and the mire. He set my feet on solid ground and steadied me as I walked along. He has given me a new song to sing, a hymn of praise to our God. Many will see what he has done and be amazed. They will put their trust in the Lord.*

Psalm 40:1–3

May all who read this book be *amazed* at *God* and how *awesome* He is, and may all who read put their *trust* in *Him*.

God bless you all!

AFTERWORD

By Bob Wilson

I don't think that it would be an understatement to say that the year 2020 was a crazy year. It was unlike any year I had experienced or could have possibly come up with for many reasons. It started normal enough. Being a professional musician, I rang in the New Year playing in a jazz quartet at an upscale restaurant. At the stroke of midnight, all the couples shared a kiss to ring in the New Year, but I stood there alone. You see, I had been single for quite some time, and by now, I was convinced that I was never going to find true love. I was forty-seven years old, and mostly everyone my age that I knew was either married with families or taken. The so-called ship had sailed.

Then in March, COVID-19 hit the U. S., and soon we were on a lockdown. "How am I ever going to find that special someone now?" I wondered.

The world was now a strange place to live in. I would walk the once-busy streets of my neighborhood, now a ghost town. As a self-employed painter, I worked alone for the most part, and due to the uncertainty of the time, most people were uncomfortable getting together socially. I had very little human contact.

Proverbs 3:5–6 says, "Trust in the Lord with all your heart; do not depend on your own understanding. Seek his will in all you do, and he will show you which path to take." Whether or not it was in the cards for me to find someone, I decided to put my trust in God, believing whatever His plan was for me, it would be the best. One evening, as I sat on the couch watching a movie with my two cats, peace came over me, and I began to count my blessings. I had a roof over my head, I had steady work when not too many were working at all, and food on my table. I was blessed.

Due to the uncertainty of the time, the church I had attended was restricted to online services only. After a while, they were able to re-open. I was more than ready to go! There were not many in attendance that first day, but among them, I did notice someone who was two rows ahead of me. I only knew her as the woman who had recently lost her husband. She sat with her two children. After the service, she turned around and looked in my direction. Our eyes locked, and we briefly smiled (or so it seemed) behind our masks. I thought nothing more of it after that, and I was glad I could finally attend church again.

So, life went on. Spring was in full swing along with the warm weather, and I was able to get back outside painting, but I was not out playing music anywhere, which was hard. So here I was, adjusting to this new life, thinking that nothing was ever going to be the same. Little did I know how true that was going to be, in more ways than one!

One Friday in late June, I received an email from

Larisa inquiring about a movie on TV that she thought I would be interested in. I was pleasantly surprised that she had reached out to me, considering that we did not really know each other. I found the gesture very thoughtful, and a friendship was born. As the weeks went by, we would occasionally message each other and talk a little after church on Sundays. I must admit that after a while, I began to look forward to our conversations.

One day she invited me over for pizza, and I graciously accepted.

Now at this point, you may be wondering what my intentions were. I can honestly say I saw this strictly as a friendship. This was a woman who had recently lost her husband, and I was certain, still grieving. Still, I was happy to have a friend and a Christian friend at that. It was invigorating to actually get out of my house and spend time with someone. Pulling down the driveway for the first time, I saw Larisa waiting to meet me. When she invited me into her home, I noticed the family portrait hanging on the wall in the living room. This only served to reinforce my thoughts of being strictly friends.

Before we ate, she asked me to say grace. Eating alone for the longest time, I felt a little rusty praying aloud. As we started to eat, engaging in small talk, I thought she was very nice, and I was enjoying our time together.

But something changed as our conversation got deeper. We talked about books, and the Bible,, particularly the book of Revelation. At this point, we both became very animated, and something happened. There was a connection. Don't get me wrong, I still had no idea of what was yet to come, but there certainly was chemistry here.

The rest, as they say, is history.

So not only did God answer my prayers, but He did so at a time when it seemed impossible to do so!

Looking back now, I can't believe how dramatically my life has changed. I was once a single guy, living life on my own terms, doing whatever I wanted whenever I wanted. Oh, sure, I had a relationship with God, but I still had a lot of self-ambition and a lot of learning to do. Now here I am, a husband, a stepfather, a spiritual leader, and a provider. It was overwhelming, to say the least! I had spent the majority of my life doing it *my* way. And guess what? I found out that *God's* way is far better! Through it all, I learned that putting God first puts everything else into proper perspective. When I trusted God, He gave me a life beyond what I could have imagined.

Do you know what the most amazing thing about my story is? I didn't deserve all this, yet God gave it to me anyway. That's called grace.

Speaking of things we don't deserve, God gave us the greatest thing of all, and it's for anyone who is willing to receive it, and it's free! It is the gift of being a part of His family, eternity with Him, and deep peace that is beyond our understanding.

Life is short. Whether you're in it for twenty years or a hundred years, it's just a drop in the bucket when compared to eternity. Do you know where you're headed after this life? It's arguably the most important question you could ever ask yourself.

Maybe you have already put your trust in Jesus, but if you're a skeptic, ask God to reveal Himself to you. Jeremiah 29:13 says, "If you look for me wholeheartedly, you will find me." If nothing else, it's worth considering! I can speak from experience that this works.

If you're ready to become a part of God's family today, tell Him! Say something like: "God, I can't do this on my own. I need You. Forgive me for all my wrongdoings. I accept Jesus as my Lord and Savior. I want to be a part of Your family. Amen."

Jesus promises that "everyone who lives in me and believes in me will never ever die" (John 11:26). Now, what could be better than that?

CPSIA information can be obtained
at www.ICGtesting.com
Printed in the USA
BVHW030628230722
642852BV00012B/201